Social Justice

Welfare, Crime and Society

Edited by Janet Newman and Nicola Yeates

Open University Press in association with The Open University

Open University Press
McGraw-Hill Education
McGraw-Hill House
Shoppenhangers Road
Maidenhead
Berkshire
England
SL6 2QL

Email: enquiries@openup.co.uk
world wide web: www.openup.co.uk

and Two Penn Plaza, New York, NY 10121-2289, USA

First published 2008

A catalogue record of this book is available from the British Library

ISBN 0 3352 2930 1 *paperback*

ISBN 978 0 3352 2930 7 *paperback*

ISBN 0 3352 2929 8 *hardback*

ISBN 978 0 3352 2929 1 *hardback*

Library of Congress Cataloguing-in-Publication Data

CIP data applied for

Edited and designed by The Open University.

Typeset in India by Alden Prepress Services, Chennai.

Printed and bound in the United Kingdom by Alden Group, Oxfordshire.

1.1

Social Justice
Welfare, Crime and Soci

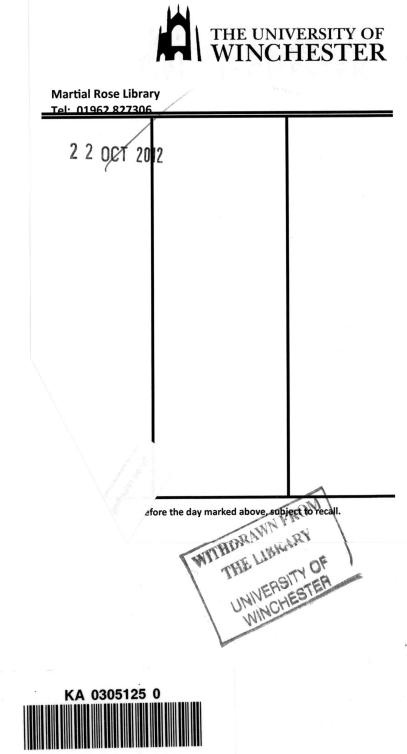

THE UNIVERSITY OF
WINCHESTER

Martial Rose Library
Tel: 01962 827306

2 2 OCT 2012

This book is part of a series published by Open University Press in association with The Open University. The three books in the Welfare, Crime and Society series are:

Social Justice: Welfare, Crime and Society (edited by Janet Newman and Nicola Yeates)

Security: Welfare, Crime and Society (edited by Allan Cochrane and Deborah Talbot)

Community: Welfare, Crime and Society (edited by Gerry Mooney and Sarah Neal)

This publication forms part of the Open University course *Welfare, crime and society* (DD208). Details of this and other Open University courses can be obtained from the Student Registration and Enquiry Service, The Open University, PO Box 197, Milton Keynes, MK7 6BJ, United Kingdom; tel. +44 (0)845 300 6090; email general-enquiries@open.ac.uk.

Alternatively, you may visit The Open University website at http://www.open.ac.uk where you can learn more about the wide range of courses and packs offered at all levels by The Open University.

To purchase a selection of Open University course materials visit http://www.ouw.co.uk, or contact Open University Worldwide Ltd, Walton Hall, Milton Keynes MK7 6AA, United Kingdom for a brochure, tel. +44 (0)1908 858785; fax +44 (0)1908 858787; email ouw-customer-services@open.ac.uk

Contents

Notes on contributors

John Clarke is Professor of Social Policy at The Open University. His recent books include *Changing Welfare, Changing States* (Sage, 2004) and *Creating Citizen-Consumers: Changing Publics and Changing Public Services* (with Janet Newman; Sage, 2007). He is currently writing *Publics, Politics and Power: Remaking the Public in Public Services* (with Janet Newman; Sage, 2009).

Allan Cochrane is Professor of Urban Studies at The Open University. He is author of *Understanding Urban Policy* (Blackwell, 2007) and (with John Allen and Doreen Massey) of *Rethinking the Region* (Routledge, 1998), as well as editor (with John Clarke and Sharon Gewirtz) of *Comparing Welfare States* (Sage, 2001).

Gerry Mooney is Senior Lecturer in Social Policy and Staff Tutor, Social Sciences, at The Open University in Scotland. He is co-author of *Rethinking Welfare* (Sage, 2002) and co-editor of *Exploring Social Policy in the 'New' Scotland* (The Policy Press, 2005) and *New Labour/Hard Labour?* (The Policy Press, 2007).

Sarah Neal is Senior Lecturer in Social Policy at The Open University. Her books include *The Making of Equal Opportunities Policies in Universities* (Open University Press, 1998); *The New Countryside: Ethnicity, Nation and Exclusion in Contemporary Rural Britain* (edited with Julian Agyeman; The Policy Press, 2006); *Rural Identities: Ethnicity and Community in the Contemporary English Countryside* (Ashgate, 2008) and *Race, Multiculture and Social Policy* (Palgrave Macmillan, 2010).

Janet Newman is Professor of Social Policy at The Open University. Her publications include *The Managerial State* (with John Clarke; Sage, 1997); *Modernising Governance: New Labour, Policy and Society* (Sage, 2001); *Remaking Governance: Peoples, Politics and the Public Sphere* (The Policy Press, 2005); *Power, Participation and Political Renewal* (with Marian Barnes and Helen Sullivan; The Policy Press, 2007) and *Creating Citizen-consumers: Changing Publics and Changing Public Services* (with John Clarke et al.; Sage, 2007).

Reece Walters is Professor of Criminology at The Open University. He has published widely in the areas of environmental crime, crimes of the powerful and sociology of criminological knowledge. His books include *Eco-crime and Genetically Modified Food* (Routledge, 2008), and *Deviant Knowledge, Criminology, Politics and Policy* (Willan, 2003). His is editorial board member of three international journals including the *British Journal of Criminology* (Oxford), and was the recent recipient of the Radzinowicz Prize in Criminology.

Beth Widdowson is Lecturer in Social Policy and Staff Tutor, Social Sciences, at The Open University. She has conducted research commissioned by the British Trade Union Congress and has held a Robert Menzies Scholarship based at Melbourne University. Her publications include work on gender, workplace violence and retirement policies, and she is currently exploring issues raised by virtual learning environments and the open education resource movement.

Nicola Yeates is Senior Lecturer in Social Policy at The Open University. Her recent books include *Globalisation and Social Policy* (Sage, 2001), *Understanding Global Social Policy* (The Policy Press, 2008) and *Migrant Workers and Globalising Care Economies: Explorations in Global Care Chains* (Palgrave Macmillan, 2009). She is co-editor of *Global Social Policy: an interdisciplinary journal of public policy and social development* (Sage) and a member of the international advisory board of *Translocations: Irish migration, race and social transformation review* (www.imrstr.dcu.ie).

Series preface

Social Justice: Welfare, Crime and Society is the first of three books in a new series of textbooks published by Open University Press in association with The Open University. The series, entitled *Welfare, Crime and Society*, is designed to provide a social scientific understanding of the complex and fascinating entanglements between the worlds of social welfare and crime control. At the heart of the series is the suggestion that it is difficult to draw a clear line between social welfare and crime control. These entanglements are examined in respect of ideas, institutions, policies and practices – and their effects and impacts. The series extends beyond national borders to look at other societies and the policy concerns and developments that link them to present-day United Kingdom. The series uses different sources of evidence to understand these trends and their effects, and it examines how evidence is mobilised in the course of research, evaluation and policymaking.

The three books in this series are as follows:

- *Social Justice: Welfare, Crime and Society*, edited by Janet Newman and Nicola Yeates. This book explores ways of defining and enacting social justice in the context of social welfare and crime control strategies. It examines how the notion of social justice informs experiences and understandings of the social world, why it appeals to so many people as a mobilising ideal for social change and policy reform, and how it shapes claims, demands and actions people take in the pursuit of the 'good society'.

- *Security: Welfare, Crime and Society*, edited by Allan Cochrane and Deborah Talbot. This book focuses on the ways in which security as an idea, an ideal and a practice can shed light on the entanglements and intersections between welfare and crime, and the ambiguities, tensions and contradictions that arise from them. The book is concerned specifically with the increasingly blurred area between social welfare and crime control policies and the ways in which it is managed.

- *Community: Welfare, Crime and Society*, edited by Gerry Mooney and Sarah Neal. At the heart of this book is an examination of the unique ability of the idea of community to work effectively as shorthand for collective well-being and positive social relations, and as a means of categorising social problems and 'problem populations'. It is this paradox that makes the idea of community a valuable lens for understanding the diverse and complex ways in which social welfare policies and crime control policies collide.

Each book is self-contained and can be read on its own or studied as part of a wide range of courses in universities and colleges. Because these books are integral elements of an Open University course (*Welfare, crime and society*), they are designed as interactive teaching texts to meet the needs of distance learners. The chapters form a planned sequence: each chapter builds on its predecessors. References backwards and forwards to other books and book chapters in the series are highlighted in bold type. Each chapter concludes with a set of suggestions for further reading in relation to its core topics. The chapters are also organised around a number of student-friendly exercises that encourage active learning:

- *Activities*: highlighted in colour, these are exercises which invite the reader to take an active part in working on the text and are intended to develop understanding and reflective analysis;

■ *Comments*: these provide feedback from the chapter's author(s) on the activities and enable the reader to compare their responses with the thoughts of the author(s).

The production of this book, and the two others that make up the series, draws on the expertise of a wide range of people beyond its editors and authors. Each book reflects the combined efforts of an Open University course team: the 'collective teacher' at the heart of the Open University's educational system. The Open University academics on the *Welfare, crime and society* course team are mainly based in the Department of Social Policy and Criminology in the Faculty of Social Sciences. Each chapter in these books has been through a thorough process of drafting and review to refine both its contents and its teaching approach. This process of development leaves us indebted to the consultant authors, tutor advisors and the course assessor. It also brings together and benefits from a range of other skills and expertise – secretarial staff, editors, designers, audio and video producers, librarians – to translate the ideas into the finished product. All of these activities are held together by the course team manager and course team chairs who ensure that all these component parts fit together successfully. Our thanks to all the contributors to this series.

Sarah Neal and Nicola Yeates, Series Editors

Chapter 1
Making social justice: ideas, struggles and responses

Janet Newman and Nicola Yeates

Contents

1   Introduction

Social justice is an idea that mobilises people to act in order to bring about change. Struggles for social justice have led to the overthrow of oppressive governments; have produced rights and entitlements for citizens, workers, children and other groups; and have helped shape responses to issues of poverty, inequality and exclusion. This book will explore how notions of social justice are *contested* and *changeable*, both incorporating new issues and demands and reflecting changing responses to social problems and to 'problem populations'.

The aims of this book are to:

■ introduce 'social justice' as a normative concept and a mobilising idea – one that has helped shape struggles against inequality and injustice

■ examine the social basis of social justice, including the ways in which ideas about justice and injustice are both changeable and contested

■ look at how a focus on social justice can reveal some of the ways in which social welfare and crime control policies are entangled

■ provide an appreciation of the importance of evidence and help you to assess different kinds of evidence.

Figure 1.1
Suffragette march by the National Federation of Women Workers in Bermondsey, London, 1911; anti-globalisation protesters at the G8 Summit in Germany, 2007

You might wish to reflect for a few moments on what the notions of social justice and injustice mean for you. Focus on an occasion when you felt something was 'wrong' or 'unjust'. This may be something that you experienced yourself; it may concern someone (or a group of people) you know; or it may be a response to images of people you have never met. Then go on to think about what kinds of judgements about social justice you are making. Do you think social justice means that we should all be treated exactly the same, regardless of our past achievements (or difficulties), talents and skills? Is it a matter of having a fair distribution of resources, or is it about freedom from discrimination, oppression or harm? Whatever your answers, it is likely that your parents or grandparents would have come up with different examples, and would have used different judgements in responding to such questions. It is also likely that people in societies or cultures other than your own would answer in a different way. This highlights one of the central concerns of this book: to show how ideas about social justice are both *contested* and *changeable*.

The chapters of the book take different approaches to unravelling this concern. The present chapter sets the framework for the book by unpacking what we mean by social justice, and how it has served as a mobilising idea in struggles for social change. The chapter is structured as follows. Section 2 identifies key questions that run through the book. Section 3 helps you analyse some examples of struggles for social justice. Section 4 considers the intersections between social welfare and crime control policies, together with how these intersections may be changing. Section 5 introduces some of the core concepts that you will meet as you progress through the book. Section 6 returns to the theme of social justice and social change, introducing a global perspective that shapes many contemporary claims for social justice.

Throughout the chapter – and the book – you will find a series of activities that are designed to help you make sense of the text and to relate it to your own ideas and experiences. These activities also introduce you to the importance of assessing evidence. Whose claims should we believe? How should we interpret the images of injustice that we are faced with every day on television, in newspaper reports, in people's accounts of their personal lives in biographies or documentaries, and elsewhere? As you read on, reflect on the images and extracts you are presented with and think about what kinds of evidence they provide. We shall return to this theme in Section 7.

2 Key questions

In developing the idea that social justice is both contested and changeable, the book tries to answer three main questions. The first is: *how are ideas of social justice and injustice developed, and how do such ideas change over time?* This question addresses the 'social' dimensions of social justice by looking at how, although social justice may be experienced as something very personal, it is also inscribed in wider social values and norms – agreed ideas about how to behave – that are embodied in laws and institutions. And these are subject to change: different values and norms of social justice are called into play in different periods, in different places, and in different policy areas. The book traces the changing significance of notions of poverty, inequality, social exclusion, well-being, freedom from harm, and of global social justice in trying to answer the question about how ideas of social justice have changed over time.

Not only have ideas themselves changed but so have the ways in which ideas lead to social action. This leads to the second question: *what is the relationship between social justice and social welfare?* Here the focus is on welfare as a means of redressing poverty, inequality, exclusion, harm and other dimensions of social injustice. Welfare may be something that is provided informally – for example, caring for others in the home, or helping others through volunteer action. It may be provided by charities, voluntary groups, trade unions, mutual aid groups; and it may be provided by the state, in the form of social policies. On a global scale, it may be the focus of international programmes for the relief of poverty or for improving access to health, education and other social benefits. The theme of welfare is opened up in Chapter 2, and developed in other chapters. For example, Chapter 3 addresses the relationship between 'welfare' and 'well-being'; Chapter 4 examines how we need to locate welfare provision in the context of wider social inequalities and social divisions; while Chapter 5 explores how social justice and social welfare are 'stretched' when a global understanding of social injustice is adopted.

The book also examines how welfare policies and practices may be the source of injustice as well as justice. In particular, it highlights the tangled relationship between welfare and crime control. This is the focus of the third question: *how does social welfare intersect with crime control policies and strategies?* The concern here is with the difficult boundary between injustice, harm and crime. Some forms of injustice – for example, those that lead particular people to live in extreme poverty – may be addressed through the provision of welfare services and welfare benefits. Others may come to be defined as a crime, to be addressed through the law. The distinction may not be quite as clear as this suggests, however, and we will explore this relationship further in Section 4 of this chapter. However, it is important to note here that this book adopts a broad definition of crime – one which is seen in terms not just of who does and doesn't break the law, but a wider view of social harm. Broadly speaking, social harm focuses on the adverse impacts of particular actions, policies and arrangements on society; these may or may not be defined by the law as criminal but can nevertheless be regarded as a kind of 'crime' in the sense that they breach commonly held notions of what is 'just', fair or right. This approach enables us to explore different policy domains in which social welfare and crime control are entangled. We return to this idea in Section 4 of the chapter.

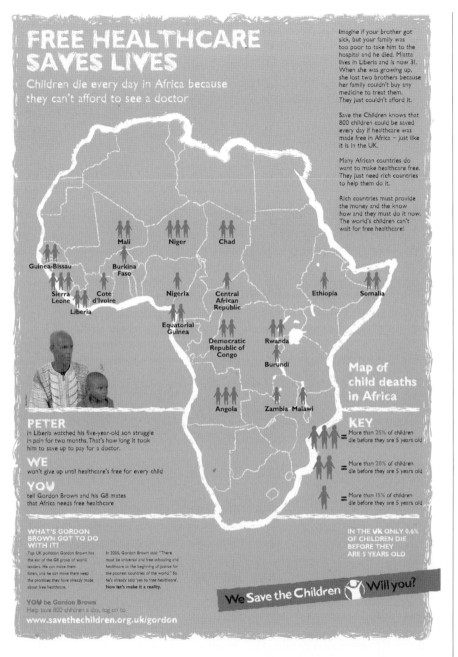

Figure 1.2
Save the Children poster

In emphasising the social dimensions of social justice, then, this book looks across a broad range of contexts and sites. It looks back in time as well as to the present day; its focus on the nations and peoples of the UK is set in the context of the experiences and positions of different nations, peoples and countries worldwide; and it focuses on how notions of social justice inform welfare and crime control policies and strategies. But first let's return to the idea that social justice necessitates a focus on the individual – their values and beliefs.

3 Experiencing and enacting social justice

In this section we focus on trying to capture personal experiences of injustice, how people make sense of those experiences and how they choose to act as a result of them. We do so by presenting two extracts – one from an autobiography, one from a newspaper – for you to read and analyse. These are snapshots of how people experienced racial segregation in the 1940s and 1950s, a period in which 'race' was a dominant social division in both South Africa and the USA.

Activity 1.1

As you read the following two extracts and the discussion that follows each one, please think about the following questions:

■ What kinds of justice or injustice are involved? What might be missing from the accounts?

■ How did those depicted in the extracts experience that injustice? How did they respond?

■ What consequences might 'felt' injustice, or the desire for justice, produce?

Note: Our responses to these questions are given in the 'Comment' at the end of this section.

Figure 1.3

Nelson Mandela during his state visit to Britain in 2003

The first extract is from the autobiography of Nelson Mandela, *Long Walk to Freedom*. Mandela was a 'freedom fighter' in the African National Congress whose social and political activism led to the successful ending of apartheid, a system of rule in which what were then called 'coloured' Africans and whites were segregated, and in which black South Africans suffered many forms of disadvantage and discrimination. Mandela wrote his autobiography clandestinely while he was in prison, and his writings on his imprisonment and on his political work are well known throughout the world. The episode we have chosen, however, comes from early in his life – in 1941, when he was 23 and training to be a lawyer.

In Extract 1.1, Mandela recounts how he was introduced to his new office and met the white secretaries and Gaur, an older black South African who worked as a clerk, interpreter and messenger.

Extract 1.1

The first morning at the firm, a pleasant young white secretary, Miss Lieberman, took me aside and said, 'Nelson, we have no colour bar here at the law firm.' She explained that at midmorning the tea-man arrived in the front parlour with tea on a tray and a number of cups. 'In honour of your arrival, we have purchased two new cups for you and Gaur,' she said. ... I was grateful for her ministrations, but I knew that the 'two new cups' she was so careful to mention were evidence of the colour bar that she said did not exist. The secretaries might share tea with the two Africans, but not the cups with which to drink it.

When I told Gaur what Miss Lieberman had said, I noticed his expression change as he listened, just as you can see a mischievous idea enter the head of a child. 'Nelson,' he said, 'at teatime, don't worry about anything. Just do as I do.' At 11 o'clock, Miss Lieberman informed us that tea had arrived. In front of the secretaries and some of the other members of the firm, Gaur went over to the tea tray and ostentatiously ignored the two new cups, selecting instead one of the old ones, and proceeded to put in generous portions of sugar, milk and then tea. He stirred his cup slowly, and then stood there drinking it in a very self-satisfied way. The secretaries stared at Gaur and then Gaur nodded to me, as if to say, 'It is your turn, Nelson.'

For a moment I was in a quandary. I neither wanted to offend the secretaries nor to alienate my new colleague, so I settled on what seemed to me the most prudent course of action: I declined to have any tea at all. I said I was not thirsty. I was then just twenty-three years old, and just finding my feet as a man, as a resident of Johannesburg and as an employee of a white firm, and I saw the middle path as the best and most reasonable one. Thereafter, at teatime, I would go to the small kitchen in the office and take my tea there in solitude.

Mandela, 1995, p. 83

We have chosen this extract to show how experiences of justice and injustice can be found in the everyday experiences we have as we live our lives, go to school or work, live in families and communities, and care for others. Like Mandela, we have to decide what our own boundaries are – what we judge to be acceptable and unacceptable and how we decide to act on that experience. In this example, while Gaur was able to confront the system, albeit in small ways, Mandela, at that point, chose not to do so, instead choosing a non-confrontational response. We do not know whether or not this episode was part of Mandela's own development of a sense of justice, but we may speculate about how far it underlined for him the injustice of apartheid and how people could contest it.

Social scientists would understand this in a particular way, arguing that a sense of justice is socially created, or constructed. This means that it is not something we are necessarily born with but is something that develops in the context of social relationships – learned from parents, friends, colleagues and many others during the course of our lives, shaped by our personal beliefs and values as well as by our experiences. This emphasis on the 'socially created' nature of justice also means that ideas about what is 'just' or 'unjust' are changeable and that prevailing notions of what is socially (un)just may be displaced by alternative ones. Usually these new ideas have to be struggled for by those experiencing discrimination or disadvantage. These struggles for new ideas and ways of enacting them are often fought at great cost to those involved. Where such struggles involve a challenge to the existing social order, those involved may be labelled as a 'problem population' and may find themselves on the receiving end of social and community responses that ostracise them, or state responses that criminalise them ('problem populations' are discussed in Chapter 4). Think how Nelson Mandela and others were labelled as 'terrorists' during the apartheid years and imprisoned on the charge of 'armed insurrection'. This was a state response to the justice claims that the social and political movements in which Mandela was involved defined as a struggle for freedom and equality.

Extract 1.2 illustrates how felt injustice can lead to forms of protest and dissent that, while initially being defined as illegal, may eventually result in changes to the law. It concerns civil rights activists in the USA in the 1950s. Those who protested against the 'colour bar' (termed 'Jim Crow' laws in the extract) that existed in some US states at that time were charged with criminal offences, and if judged guilty found themselves with a criminal record.

In 2006 (the time when Extract 1.2 was written), a bill was being passed in Alabama, a southern US state, that would give official pardons to those with criminal records. This was reported in *The Guardian* newspaper as follows.

Extract 1.2

It is nearly 55 years since Lillie Mae Bradford was charged with 'disorderly conduct' for sitting in the whites-only seats on an Alabama bus, and she is still waiting for a pardon.

A lot has changed in Alabama since that day in May 1951. The civil rights movement took off and when another black woman from Montgomery, Rosa Parks, followed Ms Bradford's example more than four years later, her arrest provoked a bus boycott that marked the beginning of the end for segregation in the South. ... She became a civil rights icon, and when she died last October her body lay in state in Congress in Washington, a tribute normally reserved for presidents.

Only afterwards was it widely reported that Parks had died with a police record – and that thousands of other black southerners had similar records – for disobeying racist laws.

So while the South abolished Jim Crow (the epithet, derived from a minstrel show character, given to the segregation laws) and claimed to move on, a large number of African Americans were left carrying its burden decades later. Ms Bradford felt it every time she applied for a government job.

'There was always a box that said: Do you have a criminal record?' she recalled. 'I went for federal clerk positions, and I would pass the tests, but I wouldn't get the job. That's when I came to the conclusion that it was because I had a police record.'

Many others with criminal records for resisting Jim Crow laws later had difficulty in getting a mortgage and throughout their lives were never quite treated as full citizens. Until three years ago, anyone with a felony on their records was unable to vote.

Today, the Alabama senate is expected to vote on a bill aimed at setting the record straight. ... But not everybody wants to be pardoned. Some think it suggests that they did something wrong in the first place.

Washington Booker was a Birmingham schoolboy when he was arrested in 1963 for protesting against Jim Crow and the brutality of the city's police commissioner, Theophilus 'Bull' Connor, who regularly turned dogs and firehoses on civil rights demonstrators. It remains Mr Booker's proudest moment.

'Pardon me for what? For demanding civil rights I should have had on the day I was born? Excuse me! ... I don't want to take it off my record. ... I think it was a just and righteous act, and I was lucky to be able to do it. We changed the course of human history.'

Borger, 2006, p. 15

Figure 1.4

A 17-year-old civil rights demonstrator is attacked by a police dog while being restrained by a policeman in 1963

This extract illustrates the possible impact of modest acts of defiance by those protesting against social injustice. It also opens up questions about the relationship between justice, the law and the state. On the one hand, the law is an institution of the state that embodies particular ideas of what is just and unjust at certain times in certain places, and reinforces that idea with criminal justice institutions; that is, the police, courts, prison and probation services. These legal notions of justice are not, however, necessarily shared by everyone. In addition, the state does not just *reflect* certain notions about justice, it also *creates* injustice. After all, it was through the state that systems of apartheid were legalised, enforced and upheld in South Africa, while the southern states of the USA continued to penalise (and criminalise) those individuals and communities who had been engaged in civil rights struggles, long after the laws upholding segregation had been officially dismantled.

From today's vantage point, there is a strong international consensus that racial segregation and discrimination, and the laws maintaining and reinforcing them, are unjust and harmful. But in the 1950s and early 1960s, in some US states, the 'Jim Crow' laws reflected the views of most of the white population about what was just and unjust – views that most of the black population did not share. So, as well as being changeable, we can see that ideas of justice are contested. It is through contestation that beliefs, ideas and laws change. Some methods of contestation, such as discussion and debate in the media or parliament, and certain types of actions by political parties and groups of concerned individuals, are more likely to be viewed as legitimate; other methods of contestation – such as 'civil disobedience' – are more likely to be defined as illegitimate, and to invoke the criminal law.

Comment

Before we move on to the next part of our discussion, let's return to the questions set out at the beginning of Activity 1.1. In relation to the first questions (what kinds of justice or injustice are involved and what might be missing from the accounts?) it might seem that the two extracts are very similar in this respect, both being about discrimination on the basis of skin colour or ethnicity. It is no accident that in those two places and at those particular moments 'race' was a primary axis of social division, but this served to mask other axes of inequality – for example, those between men and women, or between rich and poor – that compounded these racialised injustices. People tend not to experience themselves as having one-dimensional identities, though they may decide to foreground a particular aspect of their identity when working with others against injustice. Rosa Parks, for example, chose to protest against racial, rather than gender, discrimination. Had she been born thirty years later, she may have chosen differently.

We need, then, to take account of the context which shapes responses to inequality – apartheid in South Africa, the aftermath of slavery in the USA, and, in later periods, the legacies of colonialism and the effects of international migration. This in turn raises questions about the relationship between different axes of inequality. For example, the legacies of British colonialism produced conditions in which many of those living in former colonies went to the UK in the search for economic survival, only to experience long years of deep poverty there; and this poverty compounded their experience of racial discrimination. Gender, too, is significant: many migrants became employed in service jobs traditionally staffed by women – for example, cleaning, catering, care work, nursing – which were among the lowest paid and the most difficult to progress from.

Any particular example, then, needs to be examined in terms of the different axes of discrimination or injustice that may be relevant. You will meet other examples later in this chapter and in subsequent chapters of this book.

In relation to the second set of questions in Activity 1.1 (how did those depicted in the extracts experience that injustice and how did they respond?), we do not have a lot of evidence about how people felt, though the second extract suggests the pride, bravery and other emotions that occur when people stand up for what they believe in.

We might, however, note the importance of differences in how people respond: Gaur's protest in the Mandela extract is linked to being 'mischievous', whereas Mandela chooses to withdraw from conflict by taking his tea separately. While some clearly wanted 'pardons' for acts of criminality conducted against unjust laws in the second extract, others assertively refused them. This might help us to make sense of people's different reactions when they confront injustice in the classroom or workplace – some may decide to take on the role of 'whistle-blower' or make a complaint through grievance procedures; others may identify with those individuals they regard as oppressed or less powerful than themselves and speak up on their behalf; while others – for a host of personal reasons – may choose not to act, even where they share the sense of injustice. Responses to the third question in Activity 1.1 (what consequences might 'felt' injustice, or the desire for justice, produce?) are the focus of the next section.

4   Social justice, social welfare and crime control

In this section we focus on the kinds of response that societies make in order to overcome injustice, highlighting two seemingly different kinds of response – social welfare and crime control. These are set out in Table 1.1. You are likely to meet a lot of tables of this kind, and it is important to take a fairly hard look at them. They may help us to think through matters by contrasting one element with another in order to highlight differences. As Table 1.1 shows, it is possible to differentiate the domains of social welfare and crime control in this way, in terms of their distinguishing characteristics and orientations. Thus, social welfare is oriented towards the creation and maintenance of social well-being through the provision of various social supports, combating social inequalities by promoting redistribution and social inclusion, and countering various social harms such as poverty and discrimination. Conversely, the domain of crime control is more oriented towards the creation and maintenance of social stability, social order and security by addressing the behaviours and activities of those who are perceived to threaten these in some way. This approach also helps us to identify the different agencies and organisations involved in social welfare as against crime control and the different means and methods they use.

Table 1.1 Social welfare and crime control

	Social welfare	Crime control
1 Purpose	Creating social well-being by redressing inequality and other forms of social harm	Creating and maintaining social stability and order by exercising control over those who threaten to disrupt these
2 Policy focus	Welfare, well-being	Crime, harm
3 Policy domain	Social policy	Criminal justice policy
4 Key institutions	Social services, health, education, housing, social security, training, employment	Police, courts, prisons, probation services, the military
5 Role of the state	Redistributing resources, creating opportunities, social cohesion and inclusion	Creating and implementing laws
6 Key beliefs about society	That it is possible to work towards a better society – dissent and protest are integral to this process	That it is necessary to protect society from harm – regulation and control are necessary
7 Forms of justice	Social justice – concerned with promoting equality, inclusion and well-being	Criminal justice – concerned with promoting security and controlling crime

But we need to exercise some caution in interpreting tables such as these because they may make it harder to see the tangled relationships between different domains and responses. In the case of social welfare and crime control policies, there are many examples of entanglement between them. For example, countering antisocial behaviour may be defined as a social welfare matter in that it protects the welfare and well-being of some against the disruptions caused by others. But this example also raises wider social welfare questions: how can societies support young people and others so that they do not conduct themselves in ways that are viewed as 'antisocial'? Where should the boundary between prevention and support, on the one hand, and criminalisation on the other be drawn? What kinds of social injustice might arise in the targeting of young people as potential criminals, or in the treatment of them as actual criminals? There are no right and wrong answers here – but these questions suggest that the relationship between social welfare and crime control is dynamic (likely to change over time) and contested (the focus of debates that bring different perspectives into conflict with each other).

Activity 1.2

Think about where you consider the boundaries between social welfare and crime control might be rather more blurred than depicted in Table 1.1. For example, how different do you think the purposes of social welfare and crime control, as set out in row 1, really are? Work down the rows asking yourself the same question.

Comment

In relation to row 1, we have already mentioned the example of antisocial behaviour. A rather different example might be that of protecting children from abuse – a role taken on by both police and social workers, acting in partnership but with rather blurred boundaries between the welfare and crime control functions. The entanglements between welfare and crime control, then, take many different forms. It is interesting to note here that the people identified in the extracts in Section 3 would have been viewed, at the time, as attempting to disrupt social stability, and as a result were seen as criminals. Nevertheless, their actions are now widely viewed as bringing about the basis for a new form of society based on social justice and social welfare.

Now let's look at rows 2 and 3 of Table 1.1. Contemporary policy changes are tending to have the effect of blurring the boundaries considerably. One of the reasons for this is that the welfare state in its traditional form is considered by many commentators across the political spectrum to be in need of reform. A number of policies in European countries and beyond now emphasise improving opportunities for those on the 'margins' of society in order to contribute to wider social and economic goals. That is, they focus on creating social inclusion rather than on providing welfare (see Chapters 2 and 4). Now, notions of social exclusion are also highly relevant to developments in criminology, where ideas about an 'underclass' of marginalised individuals – often black Afro-Caribbean or Hispanic – have informed policies on crime prevention and crime control in countries such as the USA (Murray, 1984).

Rows 4 and 5, which refer to key institutions and the role of the state, are also the focus of new entanglements. Many states are handing over more responsibility for tackling crime and antisocial behaviour to local communities, who in turn address crime prevention through a mix of welfare and control strategies (**Cochrane and Newman, 2009**). Definitions of the 'good society' (row 6) are also changing, with governments paying more attention to protecting citizens from 'antisocial' behaviour that potentially disrupts the well-being of neighbourhoods and communities. This is the latest, perhaps, in a long series of attempts to control and regulate 'problem populations' – a term you will meet in Chapter 4. However, this is only one aspect of changing definitions of the good society. As environmental issues become more important in ensuring security and well-being, so attention is turning to new kinds of harm – harms perpetrated not by those traditionally defined as 'problem populations', often on the margins of society, but by the rich and powerful who perpetrate 'environmental' and other kinds of crimes. This topic is developed further in Chapter 5.

Finally, the different conceptions of justice may not be quite so clear-cut as row 7 suggests. Many struggles for social justice, including those we looked at in Section 3, produced laws (in that case against racial discrimination) that have to be enforced through the institutions of criminal justice. On the other hand, some criminal justice measures – including many of those now associated with 'anti-terrorist' measures – are viewed as producing harms such as internment (imprisonment without trial) or the loss of rights for certain population groups. The effects of these measures in turn may produce new social justice struggles. We can see, then, that the boundaries between social justice (and its delivery through social welfare) and criminal justice (delivered through criminal law and the institutions that enforce it) are blurred. The particular ways in which welfare and crime are entangled will, however, depend on how different societies in different historical periods respond to patterns of injustice, inequality and social harm.

5 Social justice, social harm and social welfare

In the Introduction to this chapter we asked you to think about what social justice means for you: whether you thought social justice was mainly about having a fair distribution of resources, or whether it also meant freedom from discrimination, oppression or harm. To help you think further about such questions, and to suggest how later chapters of this book address them, this section introduces you to some core concepts. We begin with the idea of *equality*. Equality is one of the founding principles of most statements about what might make a socially just society: think about the phrase 'liberty, equality, fraternity' that was used in the French Revolution in the eighteenth century, or the statement in the preamble to the US Declaration of Independence that 'all men are created equal'. When we look at the concept of equality more closely, its meaning is not quite as straightforward as might initially appear. For instance, the struggles against an unjust or tyrannical political regime exemplified in the extracts you met in Section 3 were calling for a different form of equality from, say, certain elements within the contemporary anti-globalisation movement. This reminds us not only that social justice is a contested and changeable idea, but that it is also multidimensional – that is, it encompasses a range of different dimensions of justice, some of which we address here.

As Chapter 2 will show, struggles against social inequality have led welfare states to attempt to redistribute resources to create a fairer – and potentially more economically prosperous – society. They are, then, concerned with distributive justice: focusing on redistribution as a way of bringing about social justice. *Redistribution* takes place through taxation, but also by the provision of schooling, health services, libraries, childcare facilities and other public goods that all have access to on an equal basis, whatever their income or wealth. This redistribution not only takes place through the state: people may give a proportion of their income to support charities which support those in greatest poverty. A focus on distributive justice – and the role of welfare states in securing it – can be linked to the dominance of class as a mobilising idea in struggles for social justice in many countries in the nineteenth and twentieth centuries, partly as a result of growing industrialisation and the poverty, exploitation and disadvantage that accompanied it. A key thinker with regard to distributive justice is John Rawls, who argued that policies designed to redistribute resources were highly desirable for the attainment of a fairer society (Rawls, 1971). For Rawls, the principle of equality did not mean that everybody had to be treated exactly the same with no regard to individual differences or talents. Provided that everybody had equal access to basic freedoms (such as economic security and education), some kind of unequal or different treatment was permitted so long as it maximised the welfare of the worst off.

A reliance on a distributive model of justice has been widely criticised. One criticism is that redistribution tends to take place only among those formally recognised as citizens, or even just among 'heads of household'. It is notable that the US Declaration of Independence refers to all *men*; it took many generations of struggle for women in the USA, UK and other Western democracies to win equal rights of citizenship. Even then, the formal entitlements of citizenship created only a limited notion of equality: women continue to be subject to discrimination long after gaining the vote. The dominance of class-based struggles in the development of welfare states meant that other dimensions of justice tended not to be addressed. This is why the distributive model of justice has been criticised, especially by feminist scholars. Iris Marian Young, for example, argues that:

> While distributive issues are crucial to a satisfactory concept of justice, it is a mistake to reduce social justice to distribution. ... The distributive paradigm ... tends to focus thinking about social justice on the allocation of material goods such as things, resources, income and wealth, or on the distribution of social positions, especially jobs. ... I wish to displace talk of justice that regards persons as primarily possessors and consumers of goods to a wider context that includes action, decisions about action, and provision of the means to develop and exercise capacities.
>
> (Young, 1990, pp. 15–16)

In this quotation Young is doing two things. First, she is arguing that a focus on redistribution as a way of bringing about social justice tends to ignore the conditions that brought about the injustices in the first place: the 'social structures and institutional context' (Young, 1990, p. 16) that reproduce existing inequalities of power and resources. To overcome this, she suggests, it is important to look behind existing social arrangements and to focus on the wider context – 'action, decisions about action' – through which social injustices are perpetrated. Second, this extract introduces the idea of social justice as being about not only the distribution of material goods but also the 'provision of the means to develop and exercise capacities' – that is, to participate fully in society. These ideas are developed further in Chapters 2, 3 and 4.

A second feminist scholar who has taken forward debates about social justice is Nancy Fraser. She introduced ideas of *recognition* that, she argues, have to be considered alongside redistribution (Fraser, 1995a, 1995b). That is, social justice is not just about who has access to resources and opportunities but also relates to whether people are recognised as being of equal worth, and so treated with dignity and respect. Such recognition depends not only on how individuals treat each other, but also on how groups are represented in, for example, the mass media and in other forms of communication. Recognition, then, is 'cultural' and 'symbolic'.

Non-recognition may sound much less significant than material inequality, but these two dimensions of injustice are interdependent. A lack of recognition, and what Fraser calls 'cultural domination', tend to happen to groups who are already economically disadvantaged; this may in turn perpetuate material inequalities. For example, the extracts in Section 3 focused on racialised forms of injustice, but questions of 'race' and the cultural domination of marginalised groups because of their colour or religion are deeply entangled with issues of poverty and disadvantage. Think back to the position of the black populations of

South Africa in the 1940s and the southern states of the USA in the 1950s. In both countries, black populations were economically exploited and suffered extreme poverty; and this poverty, and the poor life chances this produced, exacerbated their exclusion from political and social institutions. This entanglement of 'race', class and poverty is not only a matter of historical importance: it continues to the present day; for example, in the categorisation of particular groups as 'problem populations' (see Chapter 4). Lack of recognition may create the conditions in which harm, violence and abuse towards particular groups may flourish.

Both Young and Fraser, as we have seen, were writing from a feminist perspective, and they emphasise how gender (along with class and 'race') forms a significant dimension of social justice struggles. As with 'race', gender inequalities are linked to a range of economic injustices, both within and between countries. Global economic inequalities between the populations of rich and poor countries may be highly gendered because of the kinds of work in which women tend to be concentrated. For example, research by the pressure group ActionAid (2007) has highlighted the ways in which the exploitation of women's labour in poor countries (see Figure 1.5) is helping to support low prices in the supermarkets of affluent nations.

Figure 1.5
Women shelling
cashew nuts in India

Lack of recognition and respect may create the conditions in which different forms of *discrimination* and *abuse* may flourish, and (re)create a range of social harms. Here we might consider the harassment and violence inflicted upon gays and lesbians in many societies; discrimination against and abuse of people with physical or learning disabilities; domestic violence against women, and other kinds of abuse. These are not just examples of personal prejudice and may have wider social consequences: where discrimination is exercised systematically against a particular group, it may lead to problems for society as a whole. As a result, some forms of discrimination have become defined as crimes, and many states have introduced legislation banning discrimination on the grounds of sex, gender, family status, disability, sexual orientation, religious belief, 'race' and ethnicity. Such legislation has resulted from long struggles on national and transnational scales by social movements of people who have claimed that they have been excluded from employment, denied access to services and prevented from fully participating in public life. To address such concerns, however, it is not enough to prevent individual acts of discrimination; as the disability legislation acknowledges, it is also necessary to make adjustments to the social environment and to provide additional supports to remove the barriers to participation and inclusion. That is, it requires positive action, involving changes to institutions and wider society.

This section has highlighted some of the many dimensions of injustice – inequality, lack of recognition or respect, and discrimination – and begun to suggest how these might interact. We want to end it by focusing on the idea of *social harm* as a way of extending our understanding of injustice. Social harm is *social* in that it produces problems not only for the individual but also potentially for society as a whole. For example, forms of inequality such as poverty may not just be a problem for the people concerned: economic growth and the well-being of the wider society may depend on a consumer-oriented and tax-paying population. Lack of recognition or respect for particular kinds of people may engender discrimination against them, thus preventing the wider society from benefiting from their capacities, talents and skills (Chapter 3). Social exclusion may produce new categories of 'problem population' that become the scapegoats for a range of social ills, and give rise to new lines of social division and potential conflict (Chapter 4). Poverty, discrimination and inequality, then, produce potential harms for society as a whole as well as for the individuals directly affected. Social harm is also a useful idea in that it broadens what we might mean by 'crime' to incorporate environmental or corporate crime, as you will see in Chapter 5.

6 Social justice and social change

Here we return to the question introduced at the start of this chapter – how ideas and norms of social justice and injustice developed – by looking at how social groups and movements have struggled to bring about change. As you saw earlier, ideas about what constitutes 'injustice' inform people's perceptions and experiences of the social world. However, this doesn't tell us much about what triggers actions to effect social reforms. So what kinds of social conditions give rise to claims-making around social justice? Asking this question begins to opens up the relationship between social justice and social change.

Some forms of claims-making arise when widely held beliefs about socially appropriate behaviour are breached. A sense of personal or community outrage may develop, giving rise to the voicing of concerns and demands for action to be taken. When such action is not forthcoming from lawmakers and policymakers, more direct forms of action may result. As you saw in Section 3, the South African regime of apartheid and the US system of racial discrimination were challenged by collective social struggle involving the use of a variety of methods, including direct action. Feminist campaigns around domestic violence have been partly successful in changing social attitudes and bringing about governmental action in some countries; while social movements of disabled people, and of gays and lesbians, have led to important changes in the law, new employment practices and shifts in the cultural representations of disability and sexuality.

Figure 1.6
Australia's Louise Sauvage raises her arms in triumph in the women's wheelchair 800m final at the Sydney Olympic Games in 2000

One way in which social scientists have explained how the breach of social and cultural norms leads to demands for social change is through the notion of moral economy. Moral economy focuses on the interplay between social and cultural beliefs and the structure of economic activity. The notion of the moral economy is most associated with the writings of the social historian E.P. Thompson (1991 [1971]), who used it to explain the outbreak of food riots in eighteenth-century England. Thompson showed how the poor organised to take action against millers, dealers and bakers who, in raising or fixing their prices above an acceptable level, breached norms of what was regarded as a 'just price' for bread. Given that bread was a staple food of the working class, excessive prices could have a significant impact on already limited household budgets. These popular actions can be seen as an attempt to reassert the idea of justice within the food economy. While it can be difficult to imagine moral norms in another society, the principle that some people should not profit from the necessities of others – not only food but also water, air and shelter – has an enduring appeal. Of course, not all such actions bring about the desired change in laws, policies and practices, but the voicing of dissent and the act of protest are important symbolic acts of power in the struggle for social justice.

A basic condition for claims-making is the existence and enforcement of civil and political liberties such as freedom of speech, association and organisation. Such freedoms are protected in many national laws as well as in European and international law. For example, the right to freedom of association and the right to organise were enshrined in the 1948 United Nations Human Rights Convention, while the 'fundamental rights' of workers to organise to improve labour conditions were enshrined in the European Union's Social Charter (1989). Without these frameworks, social criticism and collective action would not be possible. Such frameworks provide the kinds of freedoms that governments and non-governmental entities, such as businesses, trade unions, charities and campaigning groups, have. Where they are enshrined in the constitutions of individual nation states they also provide a legal framework within which governments must act and a reference point against which policies are developed, evaluated and contested. For citizens of European countries, this contestation can involve people challenging their own government by taking cases against it to the European Court of Justice or European Court of Human Rights. This option has been used on numerous occasions from issues of social discrimination in its various forms to human rights abuses, including state-sanctioned torture and murder.

Any treatment of the relationship between social justice and social change is not complete without considering the state and the contradictory role it plays in struggles for social justice. On the one hand, the state produces what many people would regard as unjust laws and policies that are implemented through social welfare and criminal justice laws, institutions and systems. On the other hand, the state can also be a force for progressive social reform and change, enacting laws and policies that respond to changing social norms. This 'paradox' was captured in Thompson's study of the food riots (1991 [1971]). He shows that the state occupied an uneasy role in the bread disputes – while the state 'sided' with the bread merchants in subjecting some of the protesters to criminal sanctions, many of the protest actions were supported by the police and army/militia against the bread merchants (and town mayors). In essence, then, the state was caught in the contradictory relationship between the law and commonly held social norms. This theme is developed later in the book, in Chapters 2 and 4 in particular.

The relationship between social justice and social change is currently going through another set of transformations. As people become more aware of the sense of the world as a shared place, there is a need to examine what this growing global awareness means for ideas, ideals and practices of social justice. Having a global awareness means attending to the diversity of social justice arrangements, policies and practices worldwide. This not only helps us to know about ways in which social justice issues are addressed elsewhere, it also helps us better to understand the place(s) in which we live and/or come from.

Thinking internationally is not necessarily the same as thinking about social justice in global terms. Thinking globally means getting to grips, for example, with how border-crossing, globally spanning flows of goods, services, capital and people impact upon perceptions and experiences of the world as a shared place. It means attempting to understand the forms of collective action and claims-making that go beyond, or transcend, nation states (Yeates, 2008). So what difference does adding the prefix 'global' to social justice make to the ways we think about social order, social change and social policy in the contemporary world?

This 'globalisation' of perception and consciousness is expressed in a variety of ways, such as in the 'One World' movement, the idea that we occupy a common place and share common resources. Such issues will be taken up in more detail in Chapter 5. For now, it is worth noting that many of the social justice campaigns and movements we have examined in this chapter may be seen in global rather than purely national terms. Not only was the construction of the apartheid system a legacy of colonialism which was global in character, but the downfall of the apartheid regime can also be seen as the outcome of a sense of common humanity and of campaigns involving a globally spanning alliance of social actors in South Africa linked to others across the world. These used a variety of methods of contestation (discussion/argument, diplomacy, boycotts and sanctions, civil and political disobedience) to undermine the moral credibility, political legitimacy and economic basis of the apartheid regime. We also saw how this sense of common humanity and desire for justice – for freedom, equality and security – was expressed in international social and human rights law. These laws form part of a system of legal and political instruments – constitutions, covenants, declarations and charters – on issues as diverse as international trade, social protection, education, housing, cultural participation, international migration, asylum, and humanitarian aid. This regime resulted from international campaigns (such as the anti-slavery movement, or the peace movement) waged over many decades, even centuries. The making of this rights regime can be seen as one example of the idea that norms of social justice are universal – that they should apply to everyone and everywhere.

However, the focus on rights as a means of ensuring social justice has been widely criticised (Duggan, 2003). While offering protection for individuals, such protection may not help reduce wider patterns of inequality and discrimination in society as a whole. For example, equal opportunities legislation in the UK focused on addressing individual cases, and such cases could be brought by men as well as women. This has meant that it failed, overall, to redress the structural inequalities of pay and status, as well as of the underlying cultural devaluations, in which women remain disadvantaged. As Basok et al. argue:

> While we have witnessed an expansion in both citizenship and human rights ..., one should caution against being overly optimistic. The same philosophical foundation that has enabled human rights to be extended across differences of class, ethnicity, sex, and so forth has sometimes been blinded by the concrete social tensions and contradictions that perpetuate substantive social injustice. In particular, an abstract conception of human beings as isolated individuals detracts attention from the structural ways in which unequal access to basic resources is built into global market economies.
>
> (Basok et al., 2006, p. 269)

Such tendencies are exacerbated by the ways in which collective mobilisations for social justice on the part of disadvantaged groups have been displaced, at least in the affluent West, by individual claims – claims that are entirely consistent with the emphasis on individual economic freedom as the basis of a new capitalist order (Duggan, 2003; Evans and Ayers, 2006). Nevertheless, the symbolic role played by the idea of universal human rights continues to help shape collective struggles for justice across the globe (Deacon, 2007; Yeates, 2008).

7   Assessing the evidence

This chapter has introduced a number of different kinds of evidence to illustrate and expand on some of the concepts we have introduced. We have used an extract from an autobiography; a newspaper article with quotations based on people's distant memories and their more recent experiences; and photographs and a poster. Later chapters will be discussing other kinds of evidence: material from policy documents, survey data, social science research, and so on. But how should we interpret the different types of evidence? Are they all of the same value? What 'counts' as evidence and what might be dismissed as invalid or insignificant? Activity 1.3 is designed to help us answer such questions.

Activity 1.3

In order to interpret evidence we need to take a critical, sceptical approach, asking a number of questions about what 'counts' as evidence. We suggest you look again at some of the evidence we have presented in this chapter with the following questions in mind:

- Whose knowledge or experience is presented as evidence?

- What kinds of evidence are presented, and what might be missing?

- How might evidence be used to try to influence policy and practice?

- In what ways are the collection and use of evidence linked to power?

Comment

Whose knowledge or experience is presented as evidence?

The evidence in the extracts chosen for Section 3 was drawn from people helping to shape social change, rather than from those with a stake in the existing social order. Do you think it would have made a difference if we had included quotations from, for example, the white population of South Africa in the 1940s, or the police force in Alabama in the 1950s? Is the account we have given biased in some way? As well as thinking about 'whose evidence' is presented, then, we might also want to think about who might be missing from the picture, and whether this matters. For example, it is those in poverty, rather than the rich, who tend to be the focus of social science research.

What kinds of evidence are presented? What might be missing?

The evidence given in the Section 3 extracts was highly personal, and was based on memories and recollections of long past events. It may, therefore, be inaccurate. However, the power of autobiographies and other personal accounts – and of the photographs included in other sections of the chapter – lies not in their accuracy but in their capacity to capture the feelings and impressions associated with a particular event or experience. This is valuable, but we should be suspicious about personal accounts or visual images as the only source of evidence. For example, other sources might be needed to give a fuller, rounder account of apartheid in South Africa or racial segregation in Alabama. We might use documents of the period to build up a detailed picture of events. We might look at films, photographs, newsreels or newspapers produced at the time to gather other kinds of impressions. We could also look at statistical evidence illustrating patterns of social inequality in access to jobs, housing, income and police protection. If we had the resources, we might commission research that systematically interviews surviving residents of the areas concerned to ask them about their memories, using the same questions for each interview so as to build up a more systematic and reliable picture of what happened and how it was experienced.

How might evidence be used to try to influence policy and practice?

This chapter has included a number of different images that were intended to bring about change in policy or practice. For example, the image taken from an ActionAid report (Figure 1.5) is intended to help move towards changes in the policies and practices of supermarkets, and/or in the choices of their customers. As you will see in subsequent chapters, statistical information is often used to demonstrate the extent and impact of inequality with the intention of bringing about reforms to social welfare and/or crime control policies.

In what ways are the collection and use of evidence linked to power?

We have already partly answered this in responding to the first three questions. In deciding 'whose evidence' to present in Section 3 we deliberately included the voices of those who at the time had little social or economic power. One consequence of this 'personal' approach is that any claims we might make on the basis of such evidence might be viewed, in policy terms, as not very scientific – as perhaps just 'anecdotal' or biased in some way. As a result, such claims may be discounted when it comes to forming – and evaluating – welfare or crime control policies. Different kinds of evidence are regarded by those with the power to make policy as more or less valid or 'robust', as we shall see in subsequent chapters of this book.

8 Review: putting the social into social justice

This chapter has focused on what is 'social' about social justice. We have addressed this in various ways. Section 2 noted how definitions of social justice are both contested and changeable; that is, they are not just abstract principles but are shaped through social relationships and cultural practices. Section 3 explored how people's own experiences of injustice may lead to social action: that is, we linked 'the personal' to 'the social'. Section 4 identified ways in which ideas of social justice have shaped both social welfare and crime control policies. Here we also began to consider ways in which such policy domains are not clearly separated, but are deeply entangled – a theme that is developed in each of the chapters that follow. Section 5 unravelled different forms of social harm, such as poverty, discrimination and inequality, and also introduced the notions of redistribution and recognition as two different dimensions of social justice. Section 6 took forward the theme of mobilising struggles for social justice, focusing on different kinds of 'claims-making' and opening up some of the implications of moving from national to global understandings of social justice.

The chapter, then, has covered a lot of ground. Before you move on to the subsequent chapters, we include a final activity (Activity 1.4) to help you consolidate some of the ideas presented here and think about how they might be applied to current struggles or debates about social justice. This activity is also partly designed to help show how social science can help us to engage with difficult ideas such as social justice by using concepts. Like the concept of social justice, concepts themselves are not static things; different writers may use them in different ways, and their use may change over time.

Activity 1.4

From your own reading and sources (newspapers, TV, the internet, books) that you have access to at the moment, can you identify examples where there are arguments going on about a particular instance of social injustice, or calls to remedy a perceived social injustice? What dimensions of injustice are involved? What kinds of action are called for to bring about improved social justice, and which of those might be viewed as legitimate ('going through the proper channels') and which might be viewed as illegitimate – and even perhaps criminal? In carrying out this activity, try not to focus on an individual claim (e.g. appeal against a legal decision) but on something that relates to the broader definitions of social justice or social harm running through this chapter.

Comment

In answering this question you may have gone back to the ideas introduced in Section 3; for example, how personal experience of injustice is leading to new forms of claims-making. You might have identified ways in which the issue that you have considered is one that principally brings in new claims for social welfare, or arguments for the control of crime, in its broadest meaning (Section 4). You might have used some of the concepts introduced in Section 5 (discrimination and inequality; redistribution and recognition). You might have identified the extent to which the issue violates the existing 'moral economy' of the society concerned, or introduces new dimensions of global social justice (Section 6). It does not matter whether you have used all of these different concepts, but you should use the activity to see which of those concepts introduced in this chapter might be relevant in understanding both the issue itself and responses to it. You will come across these same concepts in different contexts at various points throughout the book, so you should keep an eye out for the ways in which the ones we have used here are carried across the book and taken up in each of the chapters.

Further reading

Before you move on to Chapter 2 you may find it helpful to read around the issues and ideas we have introduced here. In addition to following up the references, you may wish to consult some wider materials. The journals *Critical Social Policy, Global Social Policy, Journal of Social Policy,* and *Social Policy and Society* will offer you access to recent studies, opening up debates about some of the issues we have addressed in this chapter. They are all available online for Open University students, and through other university libraries. The Policy Press have a 'Studies in poverty, inequality and social exclusion' series based on research studies on these themes in the UK. Dee Cook's *Criminal and Social Justice* (2006, Sage) explores the intersections between these two justice domains as they are expressed in the British Labour Government's policies, while Rob Reiner's *Law and Order: An Honest Citizen's Guide to Crime and Crime Control* (2007, Polity Press) is an entertaining and accessible book for non-specialists, linking issues of social justice and social exclusion with crime and its control in England and Wales. Finally, there are now a few titles that follow the approach of this book in looking across criminology and social policy: see, for example, Cochrane and Talbot's *Security: Welfare, Crime and Society* (2008), and Mooney and Neal's *Community: Welfare, Crime and Society* (2009) (both Open University Press/The Open University).

References

ActionAid (2007) *Who Pays? How British Supermarkets Are Keeping Women Workers in Poverty*, ActionAid, London; also available online from http://www.actionaid. org.uk/doc_lib/actionaid_who_pays_report.pdf (Accessed 5 November 2007).

Basok, T., Ilcan, S. and Noonan, J. (2006) 'Citizenship, human rights and social justice', *Citizenship Studies*, vol. 10, no. 3, pp. 267–73.

Borger, J. (2006) 'Civil rights heroes may get pardons', *The Guardian*, 4 April, p. 15.

Cochrane, A. and Newman, J. (2009) 'Community and policymaking' in Mooney, G. and Neal, S. (eds) *Community: Welfare, Crime and Society*, Maidenhead, Open University Press/Milton Keynes, The Open University.

Deacon, B. (2007) *Global Social Policy and Governance*, London, Sage.

Duggan, L. (2003) *The Twilight of Equality? Neoliberalism, Cultural Politics and the Attack on Equality*, Boston, MA, Beacon Press.

Evans, T. and Ayers, A.J. (2006) 'In the service of power: the global political economy of citizenship and human rights', *Citizenship Studies*, vol. 10, no. 3, pp. 289–308.

Fraser, N. (1995a) *Justice Interruptus: Critical Reflections on the 'Postsocialist' Condition*, London, Routledge.

Fraser, N. (1995b) 'From redistribution to recognition? Dilemmas of justice in a "post-socialist" age', *New Left Review*, I/212, July–August, pp. 68–93.

Mandela, N. (1995) *Long Walk to Freedom*, London, Abacus.

Murray, C. (1984) *Losing Ground: American Social Policy 1950–1980*, New York, NY, Basic Books.

Rawls, J. (1971) *A Theory of Justice*, Cambridge, MA, Harvard University Press.

Thompson, E.P. (1991 [1971]) 'The moral economy of the English crowd in the eighteenth century' in *Customs in Common: Studies in Traditional Popular Culture*, London, Merlin Press.

Yeates, N. (ed.) (2008) *Understanding Global Social Policy*, Bristol, The Policy Press.

Young, I.M. (1990) *Justice and the Politics of Difference*, Princeton, NJ, Princeton University Press.

Chapter 2
Looking for social justice: welfare states and beyond

John Clarke

Contents

1   Introduction

This chapter examines the relationships between forms of social inequality and claims for social justice, and looks at how responses to such issues have been institutionalised in particular policies, practices and organisations in Western nations.

The aims of this chapter are to:

■ explore the visibility of different forms of equality (how are some sorts of inequality made visible as public and political issues?)

■ examine how equality and justice become institutionalised in policies and organisations

■ consider how the roles that states play in promoting welfare, equality and justice have changed.

Sections 2 and 3 look at the problem of making inequalities visible and challengeable – some forms of inequality may not be perceived as a problem: they may be seen as normal or natural. Chapter 1 looked at two such examples of inequality – in South Africa and the USA – where profound patterns of inequality had been justified as natural (because they reflected biological differences between groups) and necessary (since to change them would disturb social stability and functioning). So, how do forms of inequality come to be made visible, recognised as a problem and challenged?

Section 4 addresses the question of how claims for justice become institutionalised; that is, become embodied in rules, laws, policies and organisational objectives. Such policies might range from the redistribution of economic resources (e.g. through taxation and welfare payments) through to legal entitlements that enable people to challenge forms of discrimination in economic, social or political life (e.g. treating people unfairly because of their gender). But claims may not always produce the desired policy reform. So the way that demands for rights, equality, protection or justice are institutionalised can have important consequences.

Section 4 also addresses the issue of how states became the focus of demands for greater equality and welfare because they were both political institutions (claiming to represent the nation or the people) and governmental institutions (they had the capacity to make and enforce laws, to establish rules and to provide services to the population as a whole). This conception of the state dominated questions of equality and social justice during the twentieth century. Sections 5, 6 and 7 explore some of the changes to this model of welfare states, as

significant changes in the role and reach of states created a new
landscape for conflicts over, and policies about, equality and
social justice.

2 Social inequalities: from normalisation to contestation

2.1 The natural order of things?

Although claims for social justice demand some sort of reform or redress
for social inequalities, not all forms of inequality are perceived as
problematic. It may be more accurate to say that, in different times and
places, most forms of inequality have been perceived or understood as
natural, *necessary*, or *normal*. As a result, the view has been that they do
not need to be remedied or reformed. Indeed, attempts to remedy or
reform them might be viewed as dangerous to other valued social
principles or to the current ways of doing things in a society. We might,
then, want to think about how different sorts of inequality are justified
or legitimated in ways that make them seem part of normal life rather
than a form of unfairness or injustice.

Ideas about inequalities as *natural* claim that natural or biological
differences – between men and women, between types of people ('races',
ethnic groups, nations, etc.) – explain inequalities. Such claims link
biology to character or capacity and then to economic and social
consequences. In this account, men's greater physical strength gives
them the capacity for some types of work that attract greater rewards
than 'women's work'. Such claims – about gender, 'race', ethnicity, or
even national 'characters' – are recurrently disproved, but return with
impressive regularity (Lancaster, 2003). Ideas about inequality as
necessary or *normal* tend towards a concern with how societies are
organised (rather than with natural or biological conditions). Both
popular and academic ideas about society often include ways of thinking
that justify or legitimate the existing order of things. Such ways of
thinking tend to stress how inequalities are functional and how, without
them, society would 'fall apart'. Thus, at different times, various
inequalities have been held to be functional or necessary for the
continued existence of society. Hierarchical orderings of wealth and
status in eighteenth- and nineteenth-century Europe enabled each
person to 'know their place' and to function efficiently for the benefit of
the whole society. In the absence of such a hierarchy, it was claimed,
chaos and 'anarchy' would rule (Rancière, 2006). As a result, much effort
was expended on ensuring that people did not get 'ideas above their
station'. Inequality was thus argued to be good for individuals

(enabling them to be comfortable in their place) and the society as a whole (ensuring its stability).

Such views of social hierarchies and inequalities were strongly challenged during the nineteenth and twentieth centuries by a range of social and political movements – anti-slavery movements, feminism, organised labour movements, land reform movements, civil rights struggles, and so on. Such movements have shaped our contemporary understandings of social justice and equality. Nevertheless, claims about the necessity and virtue of inequalities for social stability remain resilient. In particular, there has been a strong set of arguments about the *economic* value of inequalities which claim that, in order to create dynamism, innovation, competition and wealth, unequal incentives and rewards are necessary (Gilder, 1981). Since the mid 1970s, this view of inequality as necessary has played a strong role in challenging egalitarian social politics and policies. At the end of the twentieth century, governments influenced by this view in the UK, USA, Chile, New Zealand and elsewhere implemented social policies, particularly around welfare reform and taxation, that markedly and very quickly increased inequalities between richer and poorer groups. Such policies were also advocated by international organisations such as the International Monetary Fund and the World Bank which widely promoted them in 'developing' countries (Deacon, 2007; Gould, 2005; Yeates, 2008).

This view of inequalities as necessary is linked to arguments that interference by governments in the workings of the market is dangerous and disruptive. Such activities are often described as 'social engineering' – the attempt to create desired outcomes by the 'artificial' means of public policy and action. In this view of inequalities, economic relations – and market institutions – are seen as natural rather than social. In this account, 'social engineering' represents an interference with the 'natural order of things'. In the end, only the institutions that preserve this 'natural order' (international relations between states, the legal protection of private property, and so on) are understood as necessary. They create the conditions in which the natural, necessary and normal working of markets and economic relationships can proceed smoothly.

However, scepticism about such legitimation of inequalities may lead to challenges to the 'natural order of things' and demands that it should be changed. Social justice claims rest on the view that society *can* be changed as well as *should* be changed; they view society not as static and solid, but as contestable and changeable. The following subsection further explores this view that other ways of ordering social relationships are possible.

2.2 Contesting inequality, demanding justice: movements of people

In the face of ways of thinking about inequalities that treat them as natural, necessary or normal, claims for social justice have to struggle to make themselves heard as claims on public and political attention. So, how do people make inequality and injustice *visible, contestable,* and *changeable?* All of these elements are part of how claims for social justice are made. Let us think about them in turn.

Making visible

Given widespread legitimations of the 'natural order of things', a core challenge for social movements is to make inequality visible as a public problem. One critical part of this process is to move the experience of inequality or injustice from being a private or personal matter into being a public problem (Wright Mills, 1959). This shift from private to public makes it possible for people to see how they share experiences of inequality, oppression or injustice and thus be mobilised to act against them. Challenging master–servant or master–slave relationships, resisting intimidation and abuse in domestic settings, refusing to be treated as someone's property, insisting on the rights of those who lack property or power – all of these have involved turning private or personal conditions into collective mobilisations that present the issue as a public matter (Rancière, 2006). In the process, such movements seek to change the public rules, institutional arrangements and policies that govern these relationships – whether they are demanding the right to form workers' unions, the abolition of enslavement, or the treatment of domestic violence as a crime.

Making contestable

Social movements have to find ways of explaining the *social* character of social inequality and injustice. They need to be able to indicate that social organisation and conditions are neither natural, nor necessary, nor inevitable, but the outcome of specific social processes – the result of some interests dominating over others; the result of processes 'gone wrong', or promises unfulfilled. For example, redundancies and factory closures are often presented as necessary, natural and inevitable because this is 'how the market economy works'. But social movements have tried to find ways of making such processes contestable; often this involves mobilising across national borders. For example, workers' unions in the USA built connections with workers in Mexico and elsewhere to try to combat employers who moved work across the US–Mexican border to lower wages and defeat workers' organisations (Collins, 2004).

Making changeable

In contesting the natural order of things, social movements also have to offer conceptions of how their society might be reorganised for the better. Such conceptions include:

- insisting that societies fulfil their promises (e.g. insisting on the actual provision of justice for all where justice is proclaimed as a key principle or value)

- challenging the morality of actions by socially dominant groups (e.g. advancing ethical claims against behaviour and treatment that contravene basic values)

- insisting that less powerful and 'excluded' groups are entitled to make justice claims (e.g. challenging restrictions on voting based on property, wealth, gender, racial identification, national origin, etc.)

- expanding what counts as socially just actions and policies (e.g. including the promotion of income and wealth redistribution, advancing rights to social protection, basic resources and dignity)

- challenging the fundamental principles of current social organisation (e.g. abolishing private property and inequalities in all their forms, together with the institutions that support them).

Activity 2.1

Stop for a moment and see if you can think of a social movement that has tried to make issues of inequality or injustice visible, contestable and changeable. How did it do it? How did it turn a private or personal experience into a public concern? How did it demonstrate and challenge the social character of inequality?

Comment

You might, for example, think back to the civil rights movement or the movement against apartheid that were looked at in Chapter 1. Both of these movements took public and political actions that made inequalities visible, identified them as the result of social and political choices, and offered conceptions of an alternative social organisation that would be more just and egalitarian. But social movements have also contested other kinds of social inequalities – from labour movements demanding rights to work and a living wage, to feminist movements demanding equality between men and women and protection from violence, to disabled people's movements claiming the right to independent lives (Campbell and Oliver, 1996).

Figure 2.1
Demanding social justice? Disability activists protest at the gates of Downing Street

3 Political arithmetic: counting inequality

One way of making inequalities visible is to count them – to provide evidence about differential access to resources and opportunities, or the social impacts of differential or discriminatory treatment on, for example, variations in health status such as life expectancy or risks of illness (Shaw et al., 2007). Such evidence is clearly important if we are to comment meaningfully on overall trends in inequality, including the speed at (and extent to) which they have deepened, and how they may have deepened more in one place rather than in another. There is a long history of efforts to discover, assess and measure inequality, and many social scientists have focused on the extent of material inequalities of income and wealth. One widely used measure is the Gini coefficient (named after the Italian mathematician Corrado Gini). This measures the spread of income inequality within a country. Displays of the Gini coefficient use a scale of 0 to 1 (or sometimes 0 to 100) where 0 would be perfect income equality (everyone would have the same level of income) and 1 (or 100) would be perfect inequality (one person in a country would receive all the income). The Gini coefficient allows us to make two sorts of comparison – to compare change over time, and to compare levels of inequality between countries.

Activity 2.2

Below is an extract from the final report of the Equalities Review, which reported on equality and inequality in the UK in 2007. It uses a chart of the UK's Gini coefficient to show changes – deepening income inequalities – over a forty-year period.

Read Extract 2.1 and then examine Figure 2.2: can you see the trend of change described in the text?

Extract 2.1

Many industrialised societies experienced rises in inequality: the UK, second to the US, had the highest income inequality in the mid 1990s. Incomes at the very top grew at a much faster rate than the average. The share of total income received by the top ten per cent of earners rose from 20 per cent in 1979 to 26 per cent in 1996/7. The trend has been less dramatic since then, but the very richest are pulling away from the rest more strongly than ever. Today's top Chief Executives are paid 100 times as much as the average worker; ten years ago their earnings were only 40 times higher. These trends have been paralleled by a widening gap in wealth inequality.

These trends are highlighted by the movement over time of the Gini coefficient for income in the UK, which measures income inequality. This grew sharply through the 1980s and reached its highest recorded level in 2001. The Gini coefficient has been falling slowly over the early years of this century, reflecting a reverse in almost three decades growth of income inequality [Figure 2.2].

DCLG, 2007, p. 32

Comment

For the UK, the trend is fairly stable during the 1960s (around the 0.25 point), but it then reduces during the 1970s, until 1978–79, when it begins to increase rapidly, peaking around 2000–01 (at around 0.35), after which there is a small reduction.

Activity 2.3

The Gini coefficient also enables us to make comparisons between countries. Table 2.1 compares the Gini coefficients of several countries (using data collected between 2000 and 2003). Note that the data is displayed on a scale of 0–100, rather than 0–1.

The table lists the countries alphabetically: can you rank them from most to least unequal?

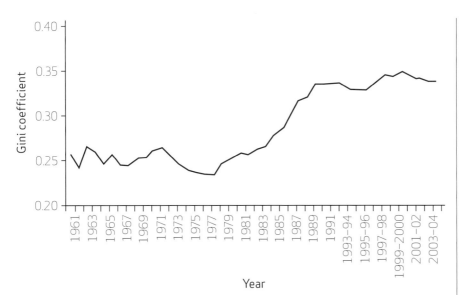

Figure 2.2
UK Gini coefficient, showing distribution of income, 1961–2004 (Source: DCLG, 2007, p. 32, Figure 2.1)

Table 2.1 Comparing income inequality

Country	Gini coefficient	Rank number
Argentina	52.8	
Brazil	54	
Canada	32.6	
Finland	26.9	
Germany	28.3	
Hungary	26.9	
Ireland	34.3	
Mexico	49.5	
Namibia	70.7	
South Africa	57.8	
Sweden	25	
USA	41	
UK	36	

Source: UNDP, 2006, Table 15

Comment

You should have come up with the following ranking: (1) Namibia; (2) South Africa; (3) Brazil; (4) Argentina; (5) Mexico; (6) USA; (7) UK; (8) Ireland; (9) Canada; (10) Germany; (11) Finland and Hungary; (12) Sweden.

The Gini coefficient is a powerful comparative tool, allowing comparison over time and between countries. But, like all such indicators, it has some limitations as a form of evidence. For the purposes of this chapter, the most important one is that it measures a specific and limited form of inequality – income inequality. Knowing about the distribution of income is important, but income is not the only material asset that may be unequally distributed. Social scientists investigating inequality argue that we need to examine wealth alongside income (Ridge and Wright, 2008). Income refers to the financial resources 'coming in' on a regular basis to an individual or household (or other groupings: nations have 'incomes' too). Income sources may include wages, dividends from investments, and money from benefits and pensions. But wealth denotes other resources, both physical and financial, that are owned by an individual (or household or other group). These can include land, agricultural assets, houses, shares and other investments. A study of the UK in 2001 estimated that the wealthiest 10 per cent of people owned 56 per cent of the wealth (an increase from 47 per cent in 1991) (Goodman and Oldfield, 2004).

What is significant about this distinction between income and wealth? A recent study of inequality in Britain put it this way:

> It is important to stress that we are looking at social divides far more important than those reflected merely by income. Many of the most wealthy in society need not work and do not draw a conventional income, just as many of the poorest cannot work and have little conventional income. Poverty and wealth are fundamentally about being excluded from society or included in it.
>
> (Dorling et al., 2007, p. 84)

Studies of economic inequality therefore need to pay attention to the distribution of wealth as well as income. The Dorling study for the Joseph Rowntree Foundation shows an increasing inequality of wealth in the UK in the late twentieth century when income inequalities grew rapidly. It also shows a greater degree of spatial segregation of wealth and poverty, with local areas increasingly dominated by wealthy or poor residents and a decline in social mixing (Dorling et al., 2007; Ridge and Wright, 2008).

Many studies choose to concentrate on poverty, rather than inequality. What is the significance of this difference? Studies of inequality examine the distribution of resources within the society as a whole. In contrast, poverty concentrates attention on one segment of society: those living below a certain level of income, or below a certain level of resources (sometimes known as 'the poverty line'). Even though poverty is mostly defined in relative terms (i.e. in terms of how much income is needed to participate in a given society), many studies of poverty tend to focus attention on poor people rather than the wider social structures which generate and reproduce poverty. In the process, then, such studies divert attention from the relationship between wealth and poverty, and the ways in which richer and more powerful groups manage to increase their wealth and hold on to it at the expense of poorer and less powerful groups (Townsend, 1979).

Much social investigation into poverty has in practice involved looking at the poorest people to see what was 'wrong' with them, and is based on the assumption that there must be something about 'them' ('the poor') that makes them different from 'us' (also known as 'normal society') (Lister, 2005). In the nineteenth century, investigators went – like intrepid explorers – into the neighbourhoods where 'the poor' lived in order to examine their habits, their ways of life, their culture and, most frequently, their character. The poor were associated with a range of social dangers – from illness, through crime and vice, to the threat of socialism (see Pearson, 1975). This focus on so-called 'problem populations' thus often coincides with a focus on poverty as concentrated in particular places (see Chapter 4).

An early and dramatic contribution to the study of poverty was made by Charles Booth and his investigators who produced a massive (seventeen-volume) study of *The Life and Labour of the People in London* between 1886 and 1903 (Booth et al., 1902–03). Booth's study aimed to combine social statistics with scientific observation of the poor, in order to provide a rational and systematic analysis that would challenge what he saw as overdramatised (and socialistic) claims about the depth of poverty and misery in London. In practice, Booth's study revealed more, rather than less, poverty than was being claimed by journalists and political activists at the time. Whereas the *Pall Mall Gazette* claimed a quarter of the London East End's population was living in poverty, Booth's survey revealed that the figure was more than one third (Rose, 1972, pp. 27–8). Booth's study gave us the concept of the 'poverty line': the level of income that an average family needed to ensure physical survival and provide the basic levels of subsistence (accommodation and basic nutritional needs). The concept was developed and refined in Benjamin Seebohm Rowntree's 1901 study of York, *Poverty: A Study of Town Life* (2000 [1901]).

Figure 2.3
Part of Booth's London poor: from Moss Street, Bankside, 1896. Houses on Moss Street are coloured black and dark blue on Booth's survey map: Black: 'Lowest class. Vicious; semi-criminal.'; Blue: 'Very poor, casual. Chronic want.'

This emphasis on statistical investigation has had a profound influence on the subsequent development of social research in the UK and how we come to know about and understand the social world. But the investigation and observation of the character and habits of the poor has also had enduring consequences, reflecting a persistent belief that the 'causes' of poverty could be discovered there. Nineteenth-century investigations into the moral failings of the poor merged into twentieth-century concerns with their 'dysfunctional' family life, or their 'culture of poverty' (a term coined by the anthropologist Oscar Lewis, 1967); by the 1980s, the idea of a 'culture of poverty' had mutated into a 'culture of dependency'. All of these terms expressed the idea that poor people had habits, attitudes and ways of life that passed poverty on across generations. This fascination with the poor in England paralleled the anthropological concern with 'natives' in Africa and India. Indeed, investigators studying Manchester, Liverpool or East London often described their investigations as journeys into 'darkest England' and used similar methods of study. Writing about similar developments in the USA, Micaela di Leonardo (1998) has described this process as the discovery of 'exotics at home'.

Investigation of inequalities and poverty forms part of the larger work of 'political arithmetic': the processes of surveying, enumerating and valuing populations (Poovey, 1995, 1998). This work has become a central feature of social science and government, producing censuses, surveys, studies and analyses that map and group the population in many different ways. In the UK, the political arithmetic of class (or socio-economic status) has long been a central concern, which in many ways can be seen as reflecting the enduring effects of inequality on British society. The class position of someone's parents has continued to exercise a powerful influence over his or her life chances: affecting social and educational mobility, likely employment prospects, and other dimensions such as risks of illness and life expectancy. Some of this impact was reduced during the 1960s and 1970s, but has been increasing again since the 1980s (DCLG, 2007). Of course, other political arithmetics have been important too. For example, equality campaigns have been informed (however loosely) by a growing body of statistical evidence about the persistence of various inequalities of income, wages, and wealth experienced by women, and the long-term effects of these on their risks of poverty during their working lives and old age.

4 Inventing welfare states

As Chapter 1 indicated, states are a main focus of claims for public pressures, demands and claims for justice and equality. This reflects the central role occupied by states as institutions in which politics, policies and resources are concentrated. States contain the institutional framework – laws, systems of administration, and processes of taxation and spending – through which justice might be enacted. From the late nineteenth century, states in Europe and North America began to develop policies – sometimes called 'social policies' – that aimed to address comprehensively aspects of the welfare of their population. In the process, ideas of welfare states entered political and academic discussion and debate.

Activity 2.4

Stop for a moment and note down what you think are the features that make a welfare state?

Comment

You may have listed issues or problems that welfare states try to address (such as unemployment, poverty, or illness). William Beveridge, one of the architects of the UK's mid-twentieth-century welfare state, defined the challenge for social policy as 'defeating the five giants': idleness, ignorance, poverty, sickness, and squalor.

You may have identified specific sorts of policy and services provision, such as health care, housing, old-age pensions and education.

You may have identified values or principles associated with welfare provision, such as universalism, meeting social needs, equitable treatment, and human dignity.

You might have focused on questions about the relationships between states and the public; for example, ideas of rights or entitlements, or provision for social groups with specific needs, such as older people, people with disabilities, parents and children.

There is no single 'right answer' here, and all of these elements feed into ideas about welfare states. Although there is a vast academic literature about the subject, there is no single definition of welfare state. The idea of a welfare state is a popular and political idea that came into prominence in certain countries of the West during the second half of the twentieth century as a way of talking about a set of relationships between states and their citizens in which collective funding, regulation, organisation and delivery of a range of benefits and services promoting social welfare took on a central role in social and political development (Clarke, 2004).

Even though the *idea* of the welfare state is relatively recent, there is a long history of collective efforts to address poverty and promote forms of welfare. In England, for example, measures to regulate wages can be dated back to the thirteenth century, while the Elizabethan Poor Law of 1601 identified and responded to some forms of poverty. Many industrialised societies developed welfare policies in the late nineteenth and early twentieth centuries (addressing unemployment and old age, in particular). In the period from the end of the Second World War to the mid 1970s, more societies developed and expanded systems of state welfare provision, leading some commentators to refer to this as the 'golden age' of welfare states (Huber and Stephens, 2001). While many so-called 'developing' countries did not develop the kinds of welfare states that emerged in the industrialised countries, they did introduce a range of welfare programmes and policies. As many of these countries were colonies, this provision was influenced by colonising countries, and the impacts of that colonial relationship are still evident today (MacPherson and Midgley, 1987; Yeates, 2008).

Figure 2.4
A factory meeting discusses the Beveridge Report (1942) *Social Insurance and Allied Services* with its author

In the remainder of this section we shall look at three views of welfare states that have a close relationship to the themes and concerns of this book: demands for equality, justice and socio-economic security; compromises and settlements; and managing and governing populations.

4.1 Demands for equality, justice and security

Welfare states have been shaped by social movements of different kinds seeking to establish greater socio-economic security, justice or equality for people. The most obvious force in this respect has been the organised working class which, in European settings, made demands on states to mitigate the effects of markets and the whims of employers. In particular, they sought protection from the vulnerabilities and vicissitudes that markets created – the risks of unemployment, sickness and old age without adequate incomes to sustain people. At the same time, demands for greater equality of material resources and opportunities produced a range of social policies, including income redistribution through progressive taxation and income maintenance schemes, as well as public services such as health care, housing and education. ('Progressive' here refers to the effect of such policies – that of redistributing from (relatively) rich to (relatively) poor people; by contrast, 'regressive' taxation and social policies either maintain or increase the unequal distribution of income and wealth.) Welfare states varied between countries – in terms of the range of social policies, the extent of their 'progressive' impact, and in terms of the relationships they installed between welfare provision and market dynamics (Esping-Andersen, 1990; Huber and Stephens, 2001). But in all cases some degree of social protection against the risks of poverty was combined with some forms of social provision, such as education, housing or health care for citizens, to provide services that could not be readily purchased in the marketplace or provided within families.

Activity 2.5

You might want to stop for a moment and think about the importance of the word 'social' in this chapter, especially in the last paragraph which talks of 'social policies', 'social protection' and 'social provision'. What does the prefix 'social' mean here?

Comment

Let me suggest a number of different, although overlapping, answers. The first is that 'social' might mark a difference from 'individual': policies and provision have a collective or public form rather than the private arrangements that individuals might make – through the market – to secure their own welfare. The second is that 'social' might distinguish some policies ('welfare') from other sorts of policies pursued by governments (e.g. economic policies, public policies, foreign policies). Here, 'social' might be taken to refer to a set of purposes or concerns about development, both of individuals and the society of which they are part. Third, we might see 'social' as referring to a set of common interests, expressed in ideas about people as citizens, being part of a public, or involving shared or collective needs. The idea of welfare as being provided through the state involves collective means (raising funds through taxation, establishing services and systems of administration) that are appropriate to achieving common purposes. In particular, these understandings of the 'social' point to a distinction between the collective institutions, purposes and policies to be pursued through the state and the private arrangements that individuals might make in the marketplace.

4.2 Compromises and settlements

A second view of welfare states sees them as the outcome of various social and political compromises and settlements. What might this mean? In Section 4.1 above, the emphasis was on movements of people making demands on governments – for greater equality, security, or social justice. But it would be wrong to think that such governments merely responded to such demands by creating social policies. On the contrary, many governments resisted such demands or, more often, constructed compromises between such demands and other social, economic and political interests and pressures. For example, the organised working class in the UK campaigned for the 'right to work' at the end of the nineteenth century and beginning of the twentieth century. In the face of the capacity of owners and managers to hire and fire workers at will, and the unpredictable booms and slumps of the international capitalist economy, the demand for a guaranteed 'right to work' was a radical one. It asked for the state – on behalf of the people as a whole – to override the power and prerogatives of owners and managers, and to construct a workable system that would at least 'smooth out' the wild fluctuations of the international economy and enable workers to provide for their own, and their families', welfare.

Figure 2.5
Demanding the right to work: unemployed workers marching in 1927

The compromise that eventually emerged formed part of a package of reforms by Liberal governments headed by Lloyd George between 1906 and 1914 that is sometimes identified as the foundation of the British welfare state. The government introduced a system of unemployment insurance (for selected trades), through which contributions paid by the worker, the employer, and the state would create an entitlement to unemployment benefit if the worker lost his (and it was 'his') job through no fault of his own. The government also established a national network of labour exchanges at which the unemployed could look for work. (The other reforms included the first steps towards national sickness insurance and old-age pensions.) Here we see a characteristic sort of compromise being constructed: the right to work was reduced to the right to unemployment benefit; only some sorts of workers were entitled to both contribute to and claim such benefits; the benefits were conditional on having built up a 'contribution record' and on not being 'at fault' in losing the job; these benefits were time-limited and carried an expectation that the worker would seek new employment. The rights of the employer were protected and the state did not seek to interfere in or manage the economic cycle. While hiring and firing remained a 'business decision', changes in the taxation system and the creation of employers' contributions to a system of national insurance (for unemployment, sickness and old age) put new demands on business. Lloyd George explained the necessity and significance of this 'compromise' in the following terms: 'Welfare is the ransom that property must pay to ensure its continued survival' (quoted in Savile, 1957).

In these terms, welfare states represent particular sorts of compromises between different social interests – in this case, between workers and employers. They are a means of constructing periods of social and political 'peace' between contending groups, preventing the threat of dissent, disorder and even revolution – a common European concern in the twentieth century, especially after the Russian Revolution of 1917. Not all compromises were shaped by such dramatic anxieties – they also became part of the way that governments managed to bring together different interests to construct a 'national interest'. The development of the welfare state in the UK after the Second World War involved the construction of a national interest in the future health and welfare of the population as a way of building a social and political settlement. Although the idea of settlements has been primarily a way of referring to how different class interests and forces are temporarily reconciled, other authors have used them to refer to a wider view of how economic, political, social and organisational systems of welfare were constructed (Hughes and Lewis, 1998). We shall return to some of these issues in Section 5.

4.3 Managing and governing populations

The idea of 'political arithmetic' that was discussed in Section 3 points to processes of classifying, counting and evaluating populations. Welfare states can be viewed as one way of acting on this arithmetic, using the knowledge generated to refine and target policies for the maintenance and even improvement of the population (Dean, 1999; Petersen et al., 1999). This approach focuses on the practices of governance, not in its narrow sense of political government, but in terms of the orientations, strategies and means of managing the population as a whole. This view derives from the work of the French scholar Michel Foucault (1991) who was interested in what he described as 'governmentalities' – the mentalities, or ways of thinking, that shaped how populations were acted upon by governmental and non-governmental agencies. These ways of acting range from simple control or repression (to eliminate undesirable people or behaviours), through to active processes of development in which governing agencies try to inculcate in people 'good habits' of self-discipline and self-control.

Welfare policies involve diverse means for managing and developing the population: social housing often involves expectations about how 'tenants' should behave; unemployment benefit is conditional on 'good behaviour' (not getting yourself fired, actively looking for work, remaining employable, and so on); and policies towards families and children promote expectations or norms of 'family life' (for instance, benefits and services have sometimes depended on being a 'fit person' or passing certain 'morality' tests – for example, see Mink, 1994). In the process, welfare policies and practices *promote certain sorts of behaviour and orientations* (the 'norms' of good conduct); *they police these behaviours* (to ensure they are being performed properly); and *they punish those who deviate from them* (e.g. by withdrawing benefits or services).

Activity 2.6

Can you think of any examples of these three ways in which welfare policies and practices act on populations or particular groups within them?

Comment

Here are my three examples, all drawn from the sphere of health policies and practices:

- *Promoting norms of good conduct:* Many governments currently wish to develop 'expert patients' – people with chronic illnesses (such as diabetes) who can be encouraged and aided to 'manage themselves', learning how to monitor their condition and their medication without medical intervention. Such expert patients embody the ideal of a 'self-governing' individual.

- *Policing behaviour:* Health visitors monitor the development of young children to ensure their 'normal development'. The work of health visitors is, in one sense, a process of surveillance and inculcation of 'appropriate' behaviours among mothers in relation to children.

- *Punishing deviation from norms of good conduct:* Recent debates about people's responsibility for their own health and the limited resources for health care have produced arguments about whether some people should be denied access to health care on the basis of their 'failure to look after themselves'. The most obvious issues relate to smoking and obesity as health-threatening conditions that might form the grounds for refusing medical treatment.

We can see here how 'welfare' and 'crime' might come to intersect in the development of welfare states and social policies. The systems of providing and administering welfare have been constructed around norms of good and desired conduct and have been attentive to 'failures' in such conduct. As a result, welfare states (especially those in the USA and the UK) have tended to 'police' the behaviour of the poor, looking for deviations, failings, pathologies and problems. The response to such failings has often been punitive, ranging from the withdrawal of access to benefits and services through to actual criminalisation. This is most clearly seen in the UK where criminal proceedings were strengthened from the late 1990s onwards in cases of proven benefit fraud (Sainsbury, 2003). Some studies have pointed to the difference between the intensity of policy and administrative resources directed at detecting (and punishing) benefit fraud compared with the low level of interest in tax fraud. Dee Cook (1989, 2006) attributes this differential disciplinary response to the fact that benefit recipients are regarded as 'takers' from the public purse, while taxpayers are regarded as 'givers' to it. Some sections of the population thus seem more vulnerable to these processes of surveillance, control and, ultimately, criminalisation than others. This theme is returned to in later chapters in this book (see also **Cochrane and Talbot, 2008** and **Mooney and Neal, 2009** for further discussion).

5 Expanding welfare: what sorts of social justice?

The 'golden age' of the welfare state was associated with movements towards equality and security that were framed by two key axes of social justice: the inequalities associated with class or socio-economic position;

and the inequalities and risks associated with the 'life course' (centred on the idea of able-bodied adulthood as a normal state of 'independence'). Welfare states, then, tended to redistribute resources to various degrees – through systems of taxation, benefits and services – across classes and across the life course. However, the dominance of these ideas of inequality and social justice was challenged in societies with welfare states across Europe, North America and Australasia by a series of social movements that revealed and criticised the normative ideas embedded in welfare policies and practices (Lewis, 2003). Such norms identified a particular sort of social architecture: the ideal or 'normal' citizen was typically white, male, able-bodied, and employed. Differences from this norm produced reduced or secondary rights and entitlements (e.g. wives being entitled to certain social security benefits as dependants of their husbands rather than as individuals). Such differences were also likely to be accompanied by institutionalised discrimination in the policies and practices of welfare state agencies (Williams, 2000). As a result, the focus of inequality struggles began to change, with inequalities associated with gender, 'race'/ethnicity, disability and other forms of difference taking their place alongside the concern with class or socio-economic differences (DCLG, 2007).

In these movements, women sought to be treated as citizens in their own right (rather than as an extension of their husband); black and minority ethnic groups challenged their exclusion from political and social rights and demanded equality of treatment; lone parents (predominantly mothers) demanded the right to be treated equally, even if they were not living in the 'normal family' model of household. Disabled people demanded the right to be treated as autonomous individuals, rather than dependent clients – a demand echoed at different times by groups of older people (retired but not dependent), and young people (as, for example, people entitled to a voice in decisions affecting their life). Struggles over the relationship between citizens and welfare states became the site of multiple and overlapping claims to be treated *justly*, rather than as 'second class citizens' (Lister, 2007).

Such developments in the articulation of these justice claims have often been described as 'new social movements'. Describing them in these terms is a way of making two related arguments. First, these 'new' social movements were in some sense different from the 'old' social movements, particularly those associated with class politics, such as trade unions and working-class parties (see Martin, 2001). Second, 'new social movements' demanded recognition as well as redistribution (see Chapter 1, Section 5). They were not only directed at changing the distribution of valued resources (wealth, income, power, life chances),

Figure 2.6
Mobilising for social justice? A demonstration in Paris by the Movement for Immigration and the Suburbs (banlieues); a Black People's Day of Action march in London; and a London demonstration in defence of lone parent benefit

but were also directed at gaining recognition for distinctive and different social groups – for social or cultural minorities who were not recognised or represented in the dominant culture and its institutions. Struggles around welfare and social justice have often combined both elements – demanding the recognition of specific social groups as citizens, and demanding forms of redistribution, including employment opportunities and income as well as welfare benefits and services.

Such movements and their claims had impacts that varied from place to place. For example, in the UK changes were made in social policies to create more equal conditions of access and provision for groups experiencing marginalisation or oppression. Laws were introduced proscribing discrimination against particular groups in many areas of economic and social life, including public services; such 'equality' laws were sometimes accompanied by the establishment of bodies to monitor and promote equality (e.g. in England, a range of bodies were merged in 2007 into a Commission for Equality and Human Rights). Finally, in some countries, laws were introduced to combat the most extreme and violent displays of prejudice – what became called 'hate crimes' (**Fergusson and Muncie, 2008**). We can see here how the search for social justice cuts across different sorts of state action – involving welfare policies, public or civil law, and the criminal justice system.

6 From inequality to exclusion

Towards the end of the twentieth century, concerns with poverty and inequality in some European and American countries were partially displaced by a new vocabulary of social exclusion. Ideas about a dependency culture and underclass emerging from the USA (Murray, 1984) again shifted attention away from poverty and patterns of inequality towards poor people. In European settings particularly, the poor came to be redefined as the 'socially excluded'. The idea of social exclusion became a key concern within the European Union (EU) during the early 1990s, building on a basis in French social policy. In France, the growing numbers of unemployed people, especially the young and ethnic minorities, were explained by failures in the processes that should have 'inserted' them into active economic and social roles. As a result, they were experiencing social exclusion from economic, social and political life (Levitas, 1998; Rosanvallon, 2000). The EU took up the term 'social exclusion' in the 1990s and made it a focus for coordinating national approaches to social development in the early 2000s.

The idea of social exclusion – rather than inequality or poverty – also became a centrepiece of Labour Party policy in the UK when the party returned to government in 1997 (Smith, 2005). The following British government statement expresses the dominant view of social exclusion:

> Social exclusion is about more than income poverty. It is a short-hand term for what can happen when people or areas have a combination of linked problems, such as unemployment, discrimination, poor skills, low incomes, poor housing, high crime and family breakdown. These problems are linked and mutually reinforcing. Social exclusion is an extreme consequence of what happens when people don't get a fair deal throughout their lives, often because of disadvantage they face at birth, and this disadvantage can be transmitted from one generation to the next.
>
> (Cabinet Office, 2008)

The concept of social exclusion has proved to be a controversial one. For its supporters, it offers the advantage of highlighting multiple types and sources of disadvantage rather than just focusing on income levels. It also makes visible the many social processes that can contribute to people being and feeling excluded, including people's abilities to take advantage of opportunities and resources (see Chapter 3 for further discussion). Critics of the concept point to a slide away from questions of the (unequal) distribution of material resources towards a narrow, individualistic and moralising emphasis (Levitas, 1998; Lister, 2005; Smith, 2005). There is a *narrow* focus on 'work', in particular paid employment, as the main – if not the only – feature of social exclusion and route to social inclusion. There is a tendency to *individualise* the problem, looking at the character and capacities of excluded people and working on them to 'improve' them, rather than looking at the wider economic and social processes that have produced exclusion. Finally, these ways of addressing 'the excluded' (like earlier views of 'the poor') often tend to view them in *moral*, rather than social or political, terms. As a result, attention comes to be focused on 'the excluded', rather than on how wider social structures and processes might produce inequality and marginalisation. 'Normal society' then persists unchallenged as the condition to which the excluded should aspire and into which they should aim to 'insert' themselves. But having been given these 'opportunities' and 'special assistance', if they fail, then they can have no one to blame but themselves (Bauman, 1998).

This last point forms part of a general political trend – especially visible in the anglophone countries of Australia, Canada, Ireland, New Zealand, the UK and the USA – towards approaches to social policy that stress individual responsibility for welfare. Individuals are expected to take responsibility for their own, and their families', welfare; and engaging in paid work is viewed as the best way to achieve this active, responsible state of independence (Goode and Maskovsky, 2001; Kingfisher, 2002;

Lister, 2005). Such 'enforced independence' is primarily associated with getting people into paid employment. It is linked to a number of tendencies:

■ encouraging or enforcing the take-up of jobs that are increasingly contingent, fragile and of poor quality

■ using public funds to subsidise these jobs

■ driving down wage levels and standards in 'poor jobs' and the surrounding labour market (Smith, 2005; Winson and Leach, 2002).

In these ways, the concern with social exclusion fits in with a number of wider trends in welfare reform that emphasise: the centrality of work/paid employment (associated with ideas of 'welfare-to-work' and 'workfare') as a means to promoting welfare; using welfare policies and resources to aid the restructuring of labour markets and support (national) economic competitiveness; and a tendency to focus on the character and habits of the 'excluded' as the explanation of social problems.

7   Beyond the state: welfare by other means

Before Western societies constructed welfare states during the twentieth century, there were other routes to welfare: self-help, mutualism, philanthropy and commercial provision (e.g. medical treatment for payment). With the rise of welfare states, many of these were taken over by the state or subsumed under its control, although limited versions of such other routes remained. Charities, voluntary organisations and private sources of welfare persisted either outside the state or in some sort of relation with it (e.g. non-state providers may receive state funds and be subject to regulatory standards). In the twenty-first century, an increasing emphasis – nationally and internationally – has been placed on encouraging a greater contribution of other sectors in producing and delivering welfare. One way of describing these changes has been through the idea of a mixed economy of welfare, combining the contributions of different sectors (public, commercial, voluntary and informal) in the provision of welfare. The reform of welfare states since the 1980s has, in part, involved changing the 'mix' of mixed economies of welfare, such that non-state agencies take on a greater role in producing and distributing welfare benefits and services, even as states take on expanded roles in financing and regulating the provision of welfare (Powell, 2007).

Activity 2.7

Can you think of any ways in which other agencies or agents are now undertaking the work of welfare that was previously done by the state?

Comment

Examples might include:

- Private financial organisations providing pensions or forms of 'insurance' against risks such as illness or unemployment.

- Public–private partnerships that raise private investment for public projects (hospitals, schools, etc.). Sometimes these extend to 'build and run' contracts, in which private contractors both build the buildings and manage the services within them for a fixed period (typically up to twenty-five years) and a guaranteed return on their investment.

- Private schools, clinics and hospitals providing alternatives to public services in education and health.

- Voluntary organisations being contracted by government to deliver services to specific 'client groups' (e.g. Age Concern running day centres or domiciliary services for older people).

- Households, families and friends increasingly providing care 'in the community' in place of public institutions.

These changes involve several dynamics. Some of them are associated with a shift *from the state to the market*, driven by arguments that markets are more dynamic, responsive and flexible than the cumbersome bureaucracies of the state. At times such changes seem to involve the retreat of the state from direct provision, encouraging competing providers to tender for welfare work or even to find customers for themselves (pensions, insurance, etc.). At other times, public organisations have been encouraged to compete with one another as if they were in a market – with hospitals, schools or universities competing for 'business' (patients, pupils, students) because public resources follow the customer. Some public organisations have even been required to divide themselves internally, separating 'purchasers' from 'providers', into a 'quasi-market' system. It may, however, be important to note the changing roles played by the state, such that even as its involvement in direct provision declines, its involvement in financing, monitoring and regulating welfare provision remains constant or even expands (Powell, 2007).

Figure 2.7

Public or private? An academy school in Manchester

These changes can also be thought of in terms of shifts *from public to private*. One recurrent political controversy concerns the privatisation of public services in terms of their transfer to private, for-profit, organisations. For example, the role of corporate organisations in the British National Health Service has expanded from the first contracting out of cleaning and other ancillary work in the early 1980s, through to public–private partnerships in the 1990s involving the leasing of facilities by public bodies built and managed by private companies, and finally to private organisations being contracted to provide services (such as surgical operations) for public funds (Pollock, 2004). However, the boundaries between public and private are not always clear: as private contractors may also receive public funds, it may be increasingly difficult to tell the difference between state and market provision.

The shifts from state to market and from public to private are key forms of privatisation, but privatisation also includes the transfer of power and/or responsibility to 'private individuals', making decisions about their own welfare – choosing how to invest in pensions; what sort of domiciliary care they wish to be supported by; or at which hospital to receive treatment. Klein and Millar (1995) term this DIY ('do-it-yourself') welfare. The process of devolving 'choices' to individual members of the public has the potential effect of 'privatising' public problems and decisions about them. This individualising process is closely linked to the process of *privatisation to the household* as an economic and social unit, producing, purchasing and organising its own welfare – from school 'choice', to 'choice' of hospital, to care for older friends or relatives.

This section has concentrated on the changing relationships between social justice, equality, welfare and the state. During the twentieth century, welfare states emerged as central social and political institutions associated with ideas of equality, justice and progress, especially in societies of the global North. However, we have seen that both welfare policies and the role of the state in social welfare have been changing. Welfare has been reshaped by more individualistic policies, emphasising personal responsibility, individual choice, and so on. The involvement of the state in welfare has been challenged, moving towards a reduced role for the state, an expanded involvement of other sectors, and a shift of responsibility towards individuals and households. But changes in welfare and changes in states are both connected to a further set of changes – changes in the *national* form that welfare and states have historically taken, because welfare states were also nation states. As a result, we see interconnected changes in welfare, the role of the state, and the meaning of the nation (see Figure 2.8).

Figure 2.8

Connecting welfare state and nation (Source: Clarke, 2004, p. 26, Figure 1.2)

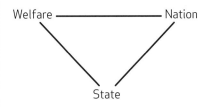

Welfare states were also nation states, and the populations they addressed were national ones. Being included in the processes of redistribution, improvement and governance meant being what Morris (1998) called a 'legitimate member of the welfare community', most obviously by being a citizen of a particular nation state. In a number of ways the national character of welfare states has been challenged, partly by processes, relationships and flows that reach beyond the nation. These include:

- international flows of capital, commodities and people

- the impact of such flows on the capacity of nation states to manage welfare problems and policies

- the influence of international organisations on the development of social policy (e.g. the European Union, the World Bank)

- the flow of policy ideas across national boundaries (e.g. welfare-to-work, or the privatisation and individualisation of welfare).

As a result, there are academic and political debates about the viability of welfare states and nation states in the face of 'global pressures' (Yeates, 2001, 2008). At the same time, there are intense conflicts about nationality and welfare 'rights': who can legitimately claim to be part of the 'nation' (and thus have access to welfare benefits and services)? To what extent can, and should, welfare rights be 'portable' (e.g. as people move between EU member states to live and work)? Can social justice claims only work within national systems? There is increasing interest in questions of equality, rights and justice that reach beyond national boundaries. In many ways, then, what was a 'taken-for-granted' framing of equality, justice and welfare questions within national limits has come under increasing challenge – involving new movements, new claims about rights, and new conceptions of social justice. These issues are taken up in Chapter 5 which looks at what it means to extend questions about social justice beyond the boundaries of the nation state.

8 Review: equality, justice and welfare states

In this chapter, we have encountered some important questions of evidence. We have looked at some statistical data on aspects of inequality (income and wealth). Such data – in the form of the Gini coefficient – enabled us to make comparison over time (in the UK) and between societies. We have also considered the limitations of using data solely about income to assess socio-economic inequality, pointing to the difference between wealth and income. Such data forms part of 'political arithmetic' – the surveying of populations to categorise and assess them – and is one of the means of making inequalities visible and contestable.

We have also seen that, for many researchers – from the nineteenth-century observers of poor people in England and 'native' populations in the colonies onwards – statistical data was, by itself, not enough. More qualitative kinds of evidence involving investigations into the character, culture or habits of 'the poor' were also a powerful means of providing evidence about poverty, indicating how reform or improvement might be accomplished. The long history of trying to assess and evaluate the character of poor people continues into contemporary concerns with the underclass, the culture of dependency, and social exclusion.

Finally, let us return to the three aims of the chapter, posed in the Introduction, and consider how they relate to the changing relations between social justice, welfare and the state that we have explored here:

■ *Explore the visibility of different forms of equality (how are some sorts of inequality made visible as public and political issues?)*

We encountered three key issues here. The first involved all those ways in which inequalities are claimed to be natural, necessary, and normal. Second, and in contrast, social movements have been powerful vehicles for challenging legitimations of inequality. They mobilise evidence, mobilise people, and mobilise political feeling – to create a pressure for social justice and the remedying of inequalities. Third, it is important to remember that national governments and international agencies also engage in the process of 'political arithmetic', measuring some sorts of inequalities and creating knowledge about populations.

■ *Examine how equality and justice become institutionalised in policies and organisations*

The core of the answer is that social and political pressures have been the driving force in making claims for social justice and equality. We have also seen that such demands may become established in specific social policies (involving the provision of benefits or services, or through changes in taxation); they may become established as legal principles (anti-discrimination laws); and they may become established in the criminal law (to protect people from abuse on the grounds of their social identity).

■ *Consider how the roles that states play in promoting welfare, equality and justice have changed*

We have traced briefly the rise of 'welfare states' in societies of the North as a way of establishing forms of social justice and equality during the twentieth century. Welfare states were a means of addressing social, economic and political pressures: the need for better health and education; the need for political stability; and the need to include or integrate core sections of the population. Such welfare states were addressed to inequalities of social class, but also found themselves involved in other equality and social justice struggles around gender, 'race'/ethnicity, and disability, for example. Since the 1980s, the concern with inequality has been partly displaced by a concern with social exclusion. At the same time, debates relating to the organisation of welfare have moved 'beyond the state', opening up questions both about the extent to which non-state actors are playing an increasingly important role in the provision of welfare in different countries, and about the need to view and understand the provision of welfare and social justice through a global lens.

Further reading

Ruth Lister's *Poverty* (2005, Polity Press) provides a rich and thoughtful overview of poverty and how it has been studied. David Smith's *On the Margins of Inclusion* (2005, The Policy Press) provides a detailed investigation of processes of exclusion and inequality in London. For an interesting comparison, see Gareth Steadman Jones's *Outcast London* (1971, Oxford University Press) which examines poverty, social class relations, and social intervention in nineteenth-century London; and David Vincent's *Poor Citizens* (1991, Longman) which focuses on the production and reproduction of poverty across the development of the British welfare state in the twentieth century. For a more internationalist flavour on the making of the welfare state, you should consult Huber and Stephens's *Development and Crisis of the Welfare State* (2001, University of Chicago Press). Nicola Yeates's *Globalization and Social Policy* (2001, Sage) gives a succinct and critical discussion of how globalisation processes open up new questions and approaches to the study of social policy and welfare states.

References

Bauman, Z. (1998) *Work, Consumerism and the New Poor*, Buckingham, Open University Press.

Booth, C. et al. (1902–03) *The Life and Labour of the People in London* (17 vols), London, Macmillan and Co.

Cabinet Office (2008) 'What do we mean by social exclusion?' [online], http://www.cabinetoffice.gov.uk/social_exclusion_task_force/context.aspx (Accessed 6 January 2008).

Campbell, J. and Oliver, M. (1996) *Disability Politics: Understanding Our Past, Changing Our Future*, London, Routledge.

Clarke, J. (2004) *Changing Welfare, Changing States*, London, Sage.

Cochrane, A. and Talbot, D. (eds) (2008) *Security: Welfare, Crime and Society*, Maidenhead, Open University Press/Milton Keynes, The Open University.

Collins, J.L. (2004) *Threads: Gender, Labor and Power in the Global Apparel Industry*, Chicago, IL, University of Chicago Press.

Cook, D. (1989) *Rich Law, Poor Law: Different Responses to Tax and Supplementary Benefit Fraud*, Buckingham, Open University Press.

Cook, D. (2006) *Criminal and Social Justice*, London, Sage.

Deacon, B. (2007) *Global Social Policy and Governance*, London, Sage.

Dean, M. (1999) *Governmentality: Power and Rule in Modern Society*, London, Sage.

Department for Communities and Local Government (DCLG) (2007) *Fairness and Freedom: The Final Report of the Equalities Review*, London, DCLG; also available online at http://archive.cabinetoffice.gov.uk/equalitiesreview/publications.html (Accessed 6 November 2007).

di Leonardo, M. (1998) *Exotics at Home: Anthropologies, Others, American Modernity*, Chicago, IL, University of Chicago Press.

Dorling, D., Rigby, J., Wheeler, B., Ballas, D., Thomas, B., Fahmy, E., Gordon, D. and Lupton, R. (2007) *Poverty, Wealth and Place in Britain, 1968 to 2005*, York, Joseph Rowntree Foundation.

Esping-Andersen, G. (1990) *Three Worlds of Welfare Capitalism*, Cambridge, Polity Press.

Fergusson, R. and Muncie, J. (2008) 'Criminalising conduct?' in Cochrane, A. and Talbot, D. (eds) (2008) *Security: Welfare, Crime and Society*, Maidenhead, Open University Press/Milton Keynes, The Open University.

Foucault, M. (1991) 'Governmentality' in Burchell, G., Gordon, C. and Miller, P. (eds) *The Foucault Effect: Studies in Governmentality*, London, Harvester Wheatsheaf.

Gilder, G. (1981) *Wealth and Poverty*, New York, NY, Basic Books.

Goode, J. and Maskovsky, J. (eds) (2001) *The New Poverty Studies: The Ethnography of Power, Politics and Impoverished People in the United States*, New York, NY, New York University Press.

Goodman, A. and Oldfield, Z. (2004) *Permanent Differences? Income and Expenditure Inequality in the 1990s and 2000s*, IFS Report No. 66, London, Institute for Fiscal Studies.

Gould, J. (ed.) (2005) *The New Conditionality: The Politics of Poverty Reduction Strategies*, London, Zed Books.

Huber, E. and Stephens, J. (2001) *Development and Crisis of the Welfare State: Parties and Policies in Global Markets*, Chicago, IL, University of Chicago Press.

Hughes, G. and Lewis, G. (eds) (1998) *Unsettling Welfare: The Reconstruction of Social Policy*, London, Routledge/Milton Keynes, The Open University.

Kingfisher, C. (ed.) (2002) *Western Welfare in Decline: Globalization and Women's Poverty*, Philadelphia, PA, University of Pennsylvania Press.

Klein, R. and Millar, J. (1995) 'Do-it-yourself social policy: searching for a new paradigm', *Social Policy and Administration*, vol. 29, no. 4, pp. 303–16.

Lancaster, R. (2003) *The Trouble with Nature: Sex in Science and Popular Culture*, San Francisco, CA, University of California Press.

Levitas, R. (1998) *The Inclusive Society? Social Exclusion and New Labour*, Basingstoke, Palgrave Macmillan.

Lewis, G. (2003) '"Difference" and social policy' in Ellison, N. and Pierson, C. (eds) *Developments in British Social Policy 2*, Basingstoke, Palgrave Macmillan.

Lewis, O. (1967) *La Vida*, London, Secker and Warburg.

Lister, R. (2005) *Poverty*, Cambridge, Polity Press.

Lister, R. (2007) 'Inclusive citizenship: realizing the potential', *Citizenship Studies*, vol. 11, no. 1, pp. 49–61.

MacPherson, S. and Midgley, J. (1987) *Comparative Social Policy and the Third World*, Brighton, Wheatsheaf.

Martin, G. (2001) 'Social movements, welfare and social policy', *Critical Social Policy*, vol. 21, no. 2, pp. 361–83.

Mink, G. (1994) *Wages of Motherhood: Inequality in the Welfare State 1917–1942*, Ithaca, NY, Cornell University Press.

Mooney, G. and Neal, S. (eds) (2009) *Community: Welfare, Crime and Society*, Maidenhead, Open University Press/Milton Keynes, The Open University.

Morris, L. (1998) 'Legitimate membership of the welfare community' in Langan, M. (ed.) *Welfare: Needs, Rights and Risks*, London, Routledge/ Milton Keynes, The Open University.

Murray, C. (1984) *Losing Ground: American Social Policy 1950–1980*, New York, NY, Basic Books.

Pearson, G. (1975) *The Deviant Imagination*, London, Macmillan.

Petersen, A., Barns, I., Dudley, J. and Harris, P. (1999) *Poststructuralism, Citizenship and Social Policy*, London, Routledge.

Pollock, A. (2004) *NHS plc*, London, Verso.

Poovey, M. (1995) *Making a Social Body: British Cultural Formation 1830–1864*, Chicago, IL, University of Chicago Press.

Poovey, M. (1998) *A History of the Modern Fact: Problems of Knowledge in the Sciences of Wealth and Society*, Chicago, IL, University of Chicago Press.

Powell, M. (2007) *Understanding the Mixed Economy of Welfare*, Bristol, The Policy Press.

Rancière, J. (2006) *Hatred of Democracy* (trans. S. Corcoran), London, Verso.

Ridge, T. and Wright, S. (eds) (2008) *Understanding Inequality, Poverty and Wealth: Policies and Prospects*, Bristol, The Policy Press.

Rosanvallon, P. (2000) *The New Social Question: Rethinking the Welfare State*, Princeton, NJ, Princeton University Press.

Rose, M. (1972) *The Relief of Poverty: 1834–1914*, London, Macmillan.

Rowntree, B.S. (2000 [1901]) *Poverty: A Study of Town Life*, Bristol, The Policy Press.

Sainsbury, R. (2003) 'Understanding social security fraud' in Millar, J. (ed.) *Understanding Social Security: Issues for Policy and Practice*, Bristol, The Policy Press.

Savile, J. (1957) 'The welfare state: an historical approach', *New Reasoner,* no. 3 (1957–58), pp. 5–25.

Shaw, M., Galobardes, B., Lawlor, D., Lynch, J., Wheeler, B. and Smith, G. (2007) *The Handbook of Inequality and Socio-Economic Position: Concepts and Measures,* Bristol, The Policy Press.

Smith, D. (2005) *On the Margins of Inclusion: Changing Labour Markets and Social Exclusion in London,* Bristol, The Policy Press.

Townsend, P. (1979) *Poverty in the United Kingdom,* London, Peregrine Books.

United Nations Development Programme (UNDP) (2006) *Human Development Report 2006,* Basingstoke and New York, Palgrave Macmillan; also available online at http://hdr.undp.org/en/reports/global/hdr2006/ (Accessed 6 November 2007).

Williams, F. (2000) 'Principles of recognition and respect in welfare' in Lewis, G., Gewirtz, S. and Clarke, J. (eds) *Rethinking Social Policy,* London, Sage/Milton Keynes, The Open University.

Winson, A. and Leach, B. (2002) *Contingent Work, Disrupted Lives,* Toronto, University of Toronto Press.

Wright Mills, C. (1959) *The Sociological Imagination,* Oxford, Oxford University Press.

Yeates, N. (2001) *Globalization and Social Policy,* London, Sage.

Yeates, N. (2008) *Understanding Global Social Policy,* Bristol, The Policy Press.

Chapter 3
Well-being, harm and work

Beth Widdowson

Contents

1   Introduction

A key theme explored in this book turns on the question of what is social about social justice (Chapter 1, Section 1). Extending the discussion in previous chapters of social justice as a contested and changeable idea, this chapter will consider how notions of social justice have expanded through a focus on ideas of well-being and harm.

The aims of this chapter are to:

- highlight how well-being and harm can be understood as ambiguous and ambivalent concepts

- explore ways in which notions of well-being and harm illuminate shifts in the meaning of social justice and in the activities of welfare states

- suggest how well-being and harm open up ways of framing welfare and crime control entanglements.

The concepts of well-being and harm are 'social' in the sense that they are differently interpreted, enacted and applied. Well-being evokes a variety of associations, ranging from our relationships with family or friends, the possibility of fulfilment through work or other activities, being healthy, having enough money to meet our needs, and so on. These in turn connect with wider concerns like feelings of (in)security (**Cochrane and Talbot, 2008**), the extent to which we feel part of a community (**Mooney and Neal, 2009**), and how much autonomy or control we have over our lives. Notions of well-being invoke the need to be protected from bodily and other forms of harm such as abuse, oppression and discrimination. However, as you will see, its application in policy can blur the boundaries between welfare and crime control measures in important ways, as supporting people to become more responsible, to engage in processes of personal development, and to make positive contributions to society can involve punitive and coercive 'sticks'.

Harm, as will be argued, is also an ambiguous concept, not least because of the problematic boundary between 'harm' and 'crime'. Some harms may become the subject of criminal and civil law – for example, rape, domestic violence, child abuse and other forms of assault that lead to bodily injury. Psychological harm – for example, that produced by the abuse of others on the grounds of their real or assumed racial or religious identity – has now been recognised in some countries in the form of legislation against 'hate crime' (**Fergusson and Muncie, 2008**). However, there are many forms of harm – especially those that arise through work – that are more ambiguous than the above examples suggest, and they open up important questions about the concerns of this book with

Figure 3.1
Different work, different harms? A sewing machinist home-worker working for below minimum wage pay; a social protest in support of migrant sex workers; and a mother juggling childcare with her other work responsibilities whilst working from home

welfare and crime control entanglements. So, how does the reframing of welfare as well-being, and of crime as harm, help us understand these entanglements in a different way?

Mobilisations against harm and for improved well-being and quality of life have long informed struggles of social movements against injustice and social inequality. Many of these struggles have centred on the domain of work. This chapter therefore focuses on the domain of work because of its capacity to illuminate deep patterns of social inequality. These include disparities in the pay and resources of those who are employed in different kinds of jobs and industries, but they also extend to the different kinds of risk – including the risk of bodily harm – experienced in different occupations. Work is also a helpful focus because of the problematic nature of defining what counts as work. For example, there has been a long struggle for recognition of the social and economic contributions made by those providing unpaid, non-waged and informal care work. A source of both well-being and significant harm, work is also important because many government and supranational organisations like the EU (European Union), ILO (International Labour Organization) and World Bank are now emphasising paid work as the best route out of poverty and social exclusion.

Section 2 looks a little more closely at the relationship between social justice, harm and well-being. Section 3 explores 'care' as both paid and unpaid work, and as a source of both well-being and harm. In Section 4 the focus shifts to other forms of work, the harms with which they are associated and the issues these raise in terms of crime control. Here, we look at crimes such as the infringement of laws and conventions intended to safeguard the human rights of workers. Across the sections a range of different sources and forms of evidence – personal accounts, research reports, films and novels – are presented, together with some questions and activities to help you reflect on their strengths and limitations.

2   Well-being, harm and social justice

In Chapter 2 (Section 6) John Clarke noted ways in which the reform of welfare states involves a shift from the notion of social equality to social inclusion. The notion of well-being is also emerging as a new way of framing policy development in some countries. What might this mean? How might it reframe some of the ideas on justice and equality you met in Chapters 1 and 2? To help answer these questions, we turn to ideas of justice that have emerged outside the context of the welfare states of the affluent global North.

Amartya Sen has argued that human well-being and freedom depend on the development of capabilities. A capability reflects a person's ability to achieve a given state of well-being by translating opportunities into outcomes such as quality of life or meaningful activity (Nussbaum and Sen, 1993). Income or wealth do not necessarily produce such outcomes; what is required, it is argued, is a focus on what Sen (1999) calls human functionings – the use a person makes of the commodities or opportunities at his or her command. This approach is more complex and multidimensional than the idea of 'equal opportunity' alone; opportunity, it suggests, is not enough since some people will need more help to achieve basic functionings than others. For example, a disabled person may require extra resources (technical aids such as wheelchairs or ramps) to achieve the same function (moving around) as an able-bodied person. Similarly, a single parent may need extra resources such as childcare, resources that enable her to fully participate in society. The government's role is to ensure access to resources through which the development of capabilities can take place. This can be illustrated by returning to the UK Equalities Review introduced in Chapter 2. Its definition of equality was as follows:

> An equal society protects and promotes equal, real freedom and substantive opportunity to live in the ways that people value and would choose, so that everyone can flourish.

> An equal society recognises different people's needs, situations and goals, and removes the barriers that limit what people can do and can be.

> (DCLG, 2007, p. 126)

In this account, equality focuses on the capabilities to flourish, and, with the help of governments, to overcome the barriers that limit what people are able to do and who they are able to be. This takes us back to the debate about redistribution and recognition you met in Chapter 1, Section 5. In these terms, redistribution of income and wealth alone do not necessarily produce enhanced capabilities and social outcomes, and what is needed is the development of capabilities to address oppression and domination. Social justice therefore involves the following: having capabilities to voice feelings and opinions and for these to be heard; participating fully in social life and having an active role in shaping it; being recognised and respected. This account opens up dimensions of well-being that emphasise autonomy, having a voice in the decisions and processes that shape our lives, being respected, cared about, and so on.

This conceptualisation of social justice is relevant to the concerns of this chapter for a number of reasons. First, it encourages us to look beyond individual explanations of well-being and harm and to locate these in a wider social context. Second, it highlights the importance of other factors, like care, that have a vital role in promoting social and personal well-being. Third, it facilitates more comprehensive and nuanced insights into how social injustice is constituted and contested.

However, the focus on well-being rather than equality has attracted a number of criticisms. Economic redistribution remains important, but it is suggested that there is a threshold beyond which redistribution may have a limited role in improving well-being. As such, the role of government in overcoming inequality shifts from one primarily orientated to redistribution to one of ensuring opportunities to enable people to develop their capacities. Having opened up such opportunities, and offered various forms of support, there will be an expectation that people take greater responsibility for developing their own well-being. To appreciate this, we need to note the subtle differences between the language of capabilities and capacities:

> Capabilities do not mean internal skills or capacities. The lack of a capability indicates a failure on the part of society to create real freedom for people: it does not indicate anything deficient about the individuals themselves.
>
> (DCLG, 2007, p. 126)

However, the policy language of 'capability building' shifts the emphasis towards the need to develop the qualities and skills of individuals and communities in order to overcome disadvantage. As such, focusing on *capabilities* may translate into policies that emphasise the *capacities* of individuals, social groups and communities. The focus on well-being therefore has the potential to redefine social justice, insisting that 'rights must at all times be balanced by responsibilities [and that] there should be no public provision for income support without a commitment by citizens to help themselves be more autonomous, enterprising and self-developmental' (Jordan, 2006, p. 131).

As noted in Chapter 2, work – and more specifically paid work – has come to be presented as the most effective way of promoting social equality and inclusion. As such, the role of welfare states in many industrialised societies has been redefined. Instead of providing a safety net, welfare states are instead becoming 'trampolines' – providing 'hand-ups' not 'handouts'. They are implementing a variety of 'welfare-to-work' policies geared toward 'activating' (promoting the labour market engagement of) socially excluded groups and building their capacities to engage in paid work. We can consider this by returning to the UK Equalities Review (DCLG, 2007).

Figure 3.2
Tony Blair – then the
UK Prime Minister –
launching a new
welfare-to-work
initiative

Activity 3.1

As you read Extract 3.1, reflect on the following questions:

■ What types of work does the extract include and exclude?

■ What connections does it make between well-being, work and social justice?

Extract 3.1

Work remains the best and fastest route out of poverty. It is the most reliable way for an individual to achieve economic independence and prosperity. ... By contrast, the absence of work is the surest route to a spiral of demoralisation, loss of motivation, skills and self-confidence, worsening health and well-being for the individual. ...

... We have the highest employment rate among the world's major industrialised economies, at 75 per cent, and boast a realistic aspiration to reach 80 per cent.

Government programmes set up to achieve this important target have progressively focused on different groups including the unemployed, ethnic minorities and disabled people. More recently the Government has published further proposals focusing on increasing the employment rates of lone parents and older people.

DCLG, 2007, p. 62

Comment

This extract places great emphasis on the potential of *paid* work to deliver a range of benefits for the individual and society. Not only does this ignore the ability of other types of work such as voluntary work and care work to produce such benefits, but the capabilities of 'socially excluded' groups are firmly linked to their capacity to participate in the formal labour market. As such, these groups become the targets of 'welfare-to-work' policies that link their personal development to participation in paid employment. These policies are, however, not simply about providing various inducements and rewards, as there are often conditionalities attached to them. In the UK, for example, receipt of Jobseeker's Allowance requires claimants to demonstrate they are capable of work, actively searching for work and available for whatever work they are offered – even if they deem that work is unsuitable given their skills and experience, or if the pay is too low to meet their needs. These policies also have a punitive and coercive dimension in that sanctions – such as the reduction or withdrawal of benefit – can be applied should the claimant not fulfil the work requirement conditions. In this way, the rhetoric of enhanced well-being resulting from taking paid work co-exists with measures that discipline claimants and punish them for failing to 'do the right thing' (Heron and Dwyer, 1999).

The extract also portrays paid work as inherently beneficial. This overlooks important questions about the quality, safeguards and social relations that mediate experiences of paid employment. So, for example, a number of sociological studies have explored how workplaces represent important sites of social interaction. For example, Anna Pollert's (1981) study of women factory workers shows how their everyday working lives are peppered by hoots of laughter as the women share anecdotes about home lives, husbands and sex. They also indicate how participating in paid work may be an important source of identity, meaning and recognition for workers. However, such studies also indicate the drudgery, humiliations, exploitations and harms that can characterise paid, and particularly low-paid, employment (Beechey, 1986; Tombs, 2004).

Well-being is therefore an ambiguous and ambivalent concept. On the one hand, it has the potential to conceal aspects of social injustice by reducing social inequalities to the individual capacities – or the lack thereof – of socially excluded groups. Such groups can thereby be represented as self-harming and harmful to wider society if they fail to take advantage of opportunities for self-development by making effective use of the 'trampolines' of welfare-to-work schemes that are designed to place them in paid work. On the other hand, the notion of well-being encourages us to think about what constitutes human flourishing, the

Figure 3.3
Open University
employees – at work
and enjoying it

capabilities through which this is realised, and the kinds of social
arrangements needed to promote them. In this way, a focus on well-
being can enrich our understanding of social justice. To further
appreciate this point, think back to the discussion of social harm in
Chapter 1, Section 5. There Janet Newman and Nicola Yeates argued that
although individual lives are often riven by traumatic events and
experiences that appear inherently personal – injuries, humiliations,
chronic illness, and the everyday struggles to keep body and soul
together to maintain self and social respect – many of these harms can
be traced back to wider social arrangements. Such harms may reside in
the social relations of power, such that those with more power are often
implicated in the lack of well-being experienced by relatively powerless
and excluded social groups (Hillyard et al., 2004). However, power
relations are complicated and they are also implicated in the personal –
often intimate – relationships involved in care work. This subject is the
focus of the following section. Before you move on to this, though,
pause briefly to consider issues of evidence.

Activity 3.2

In this section you have encountered evidence in the form of quotations
from a government policy document (The Equalities Review report),
been prompted to think about whose voice is privileged (the
government's), and what might be missing from this account of paid
work as consistently and inherently beneficial (experiences of paid work
that contradict this account). As you work through Sections 3 and 4 you

will encounter other kinds of evidence. Try to keep a note of your answers to the following:

■ What different types of evidence are used?

■ Whose perspective or voice do they reflect?

■ Might some forms of evidence be regarded as more objective or significant than others?

You will be returning to these points at different stages in the chapter, so you may want to keep your notes to hand.

3   Care, well-being and harm

Caring for and being cared for by others is clearly a source of satisfaction and well-being for many of those involved – but the caring relationship is also fraught with tension. Marian Barnes argues that:

> Care can fulfil a number of functions, including sustaining the connection between individuals at risk of exclusion and the communities within which they live, and asserting the value of people who may be devalued by society. This is important 'work' for society, even though those involved in caring relationships may not construct this in such a way.
>
> (Barnes, 2006, pp. 142–3)

This quotation opens up a possible disjuncture between the wider social and community benefits that arise from care work (in its broadest sense) and the experience of individuals involved in providing such work, many of whom receive little social recognition or few economic rewards for it. Care work has traditionally been represented as the 'natural' province of women, whether located inside or outside the household (Lewis, 2001). One reason for this is because the front line of care largely hinges on 'body work' entailing 'dirty' tasks that require routine contact with urine, faeces and human decay. As such, it tends to be regarded as low-status menial work and so deemed particularly fit for relatively powerless groups like working-class and ethnic minority women (Twigg, 2000). However, the power relations of care work are often complex, as the experience of 'Allan', who provided care for his mother and whose experience you examine in Activity 3.3 below, suggests.

Activity 3.3

Although his name has been changed, Allan is real and his story is real. His account was told to Marian Barnes during an interview she conducted with him in the course of her research on care and social justice. During this interview, Allan began by reflecting that it was only when he became a full-time carer to his mother, Catherine, in his forties, that he realised he had been her carer as a child. Catherine had used alcohol as a way of coping with the various disappointments, difficulties and challenges that shaped her life – including a number of miscarriages, parenting five children, and an unhappy marriage. As a child, Allan had learnt 'to get your mother off the bathroom floor ... make sure she wasn't sick ... and put her to bed'. As an adult he pursued a full-time career in nursing, mental welfare and social work before resigning to work freelance so he could dedicate more time to the care of his mother as her physical and mental health deteriorated. Catherine asked Allan to promise she would not be sent to a nursing home so she moved into his home after he had convinced social services – initially sceptical of his ability to care for Catherine because he was a man – he was an appropriate caregiver.

Allan's story continues in Extract 3.2 below. As you read this, reflect on:

■ What kind of evidence it represents and what does it reveal?

■ What does it tell us about care work?

■ How does it illuminate our appreciation of social justice?

Extract 3.2

So in his 40s Allan was once again caring for his mother ... His brother said he did not understand how he had loved Catherine so much. Allan described his response: 'I said I didn't ... He thought our closeness was ... you love your mother. And I said it wasn't that. Our closeness was that she could have someone in the family to guide her through things ... to minimise the impact on dad ... [and then] on neighbours ... But I didn't like her and sometimes I hated her ... .'

Allan ... used to adore going on holidays but when Catherine moved in couldn't afford it. He couldn't relax over a long shower ... because he couldn't spend much time away from her. ... He described his responsibility for 24 hour care for Catherine over four years [working in shifts with paid] carers [and] described his role as a team manager. [And] how he had had to convince the GP that she had physical problems with her ears when she was crying out in pain – the GP had claimed her screaming was the result of dementia ... [And how] on another occasion a locum nurse had complained against Allan for swearing when he responded to her 'And how are we today?' with 'I'm pissed off actually' ... He said he wanted her to have dignity and maybe come to terms with things. He described times in her final years when she would sit quietly and watch TV without a glass in her hand ...

[How] she would say ... 'I was a good mother, I worked hard and did my best for all of you' ... And that was one of her survival techniques, and I didn't want to take that away from her.

Barnes, 2006, pp. 63–9

Comment

Allan's account enables us to appreciate some of the complex ways in which care is woven into the fabric of everyday life, how it connects with well-being, and some of the consequences that flow from this. The extract undermines the perception that care work is necessarily 'women's work' and challenges assumptions about care work as a 'labour of love'. It also indicates some of the costs of giving care: the limits to personal autonomy; the difficulties of combining care work with other forms of work; and the loss of leisure and personal enjoyment. The extract also conveys how Allan's care of his mother contributes to her well-being and, in complex ways, to his own. We might therefore argue that in caring for and caring about Catherine, Allan is engaged in a personal process of enacting social justice – but one that is not without costs for him, in terms of both resources and recognition.

Figure 3.4
Care and/or control? A care worker spoon-feeds an older man in his care

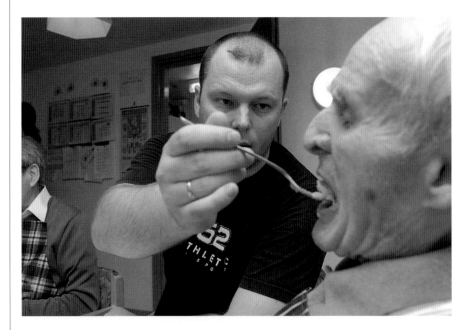

Questions of care and questions of social justice are therefore deeply intertwined, but care also illustrates the complex relationship between well-being and harm. The care relationship can embody both our best expectations of care (being attentive, competent and responsive) and worst practices (being controlling, incompetent and even abusive). The provision of care may similarly produce the well-being that results from having one's physical and emotional needs met; at the same time it may infantilise the receiver of care and lead to their loss of autonomy and independence. Look at the image in Figure 3.4: what elements of surveillance and control might be involved in this relationship? In what ways might this be experienced as oppressive rather than beneficial by the care receiver?

3.1 Care and harm

The experience of dependence has led many disabled people to voice demands for independence and equal rights. Richard Wood, former Director of the British Council of Disabled People, has argued that:

> Disabled people have never demanded or asked for care! We have sought independent living which means being able to achieve maximum independence and control over our lives. The concept of care seems to many disabled people a tool through which others are able to dominate and manage our lives.
>
> (Wood, quoted in Barnes, 2006, p. 147)

Concepts of independence and dependence are highly charged. Within the care relationship, need, resentment, gratitude, and loss of personal autonomy may combine to produce a sense of harm alongside, and perhaps in tension with, any sense of well-being. Many people with mental and physical impairments, older people, and children have been consigned to institutions and other forms of segregated provision. Nominally charged with their support, these care institutions have in practice sometimes proved to be detrimental to autonomy and welfare, involving invasive forms of surveillance, control, and abuse of a verbal, physical, financial, emotional or sexual nature (Hoggett, 2000).

These tensions are explored by a World Health Organization (2002) report into older people's experience of abuse in family, hospital and eldercare home settings in eight countries. It concluded 'that the abuse, neglect and financial exploitation of elders is much more common than societies care to admit' (WHO, 2002, p. 4). As statistical evidence does not capture the qualitative experience of abuse, a series of eight focus group interviews were held in each country in the study; six of the group interviews involved older people while the remaining two involved care workers. These demonstrated that elder abuse is multifaceted, ranging from disrespect through to the absence or inadequacy of health and welfare provision, to actual physical assault.

The report also made connections between the injustices experienced by care receivers and care workers. For example, interviews with health care workers in Argentina and Kenya indicated how they too felt mistreated, with experiences ranging from abusive behaviour from patients and family members, to low pay and the low status attached to working in geriatric medicine, combined with chronic underfunding and poor working conditions. The report summarised the dilemmas the research posed: 'This raises some interesting questions about the ability of health care professionals to be sensitive to and respond to situations of elder abuse, when they themselves feel so mistreated' (WHO, 2002, p. 17). In this way, the report makes clear connections between the well-being of caregivers and that of care recipients.

3.2 Care, social justice and welfare states

Care work, it would seem, may have the potential to result in well-being for both the carer and the person cared for – but it may also be a source of harm to each. This paradox is noted by Martha Nussbaum (2006) in her development of the capabilities approach examined earlier in Section 2 of this chapter. She identifies a number of core capabilities necessary for the development of social justice, and suggests that care is a vital component of many of these. On this basis she argues:

> Thinking well about care means thinking about a wide range of capabilities on the side of both cared-for and the caregiver ... Good care supports the capacity of the cared for ... It protects the crucial good of self-respect ... Caregivers frequently lose out through bad arrangements. Their health suffers; their emotional equanimity is sorely compromised; they lose many capabilities they otherwise would have had. A decent society cannot ensure that all caregivers actually have happy lives, but it can provide them with a threshold level of capability in each of the key areas ... [G]ood public arrangements and a decent public culture can make it possible that care ... would not involve constant anxiety about how the job would get done, and with what resources.
>
> (Nussbaum, 2006, pp. 168–70)

One way of rethinking 'public culture' hinges on debates around the ethic of care developed by feminist scholars Joan Tronto (1993) and Selma Sevenhuijsen (1998). Building particularly on arguments by Young (1990) and Fraser (1995a, 1995b) (see Chapter 1, Section 5) about the importance of taking matters of recognition into account, Tronto and Sevenhuijsen argue that care is a vital component of social justice. In doing so, they challenge some of the assumptions that surround care.

Noting how we are all in need of care, they question the presumed distinction between caregivers and care receivers – a distinction which is often blurred in practice. They also challenge the dichotomy of dependence and independence, arguing rather for a concept of interdependence.

Figure 3.5
Mobilising for disability rights

However, this approach has been contested by disability activists such as Richard Wood who, as you saw in Section 3.1 above, have advanced a rights-based approach that emphasises 'independence' rather than 'care'. As such, the claim for social rights enables relatively powerless groups to further their well-being and challenge the social harms they are subject to. It suggests that whilst gaining and exercising social (and political) rights is not without tension, social rights claims are a vital component of social justice.

Figure 3.6
Caregivers and care
receivers unite: children
and mothers protest in
support of strike action
by their local nursery
nurses

4 Work, harm and crime

Paid work has long been the focus of a range of struggles for social justice by trade unions and other social movements. Such struggles have produced a range of legal instruments to protect workers from harm and the excesses of exploitation. For example, the International Labour Organization (ILO), an agency of the United Nations, is mandated to promote workers' well-being and human rights. Extolling the virtues of paid work in ways that echo the UK Equalities Review, the ILO argues that work is vital to well-being and the promotion of social equality. Crucially, though, it inserts an important caveat:

> Such progress, however, hinges on work that is decent.
>
> Decent work sums up the aspirations of people in their working lives. It involves opportunities for work that is productive and delivers a fair income, security in the workplace and social protection for families. Decent work means better prospects for personal development and social integration, and freedom for people to express their concerns, organize and participate in decisions that affect their lives. It entails equality of opportunity and treatment for all women and men.
>
> Decent work is the key to the eradication of poverty. ... Extending opportunities for decent work to people is a crucial element in making [societies] more inclusive and fair.
>
> (ILO, 2007, p. 3)

That is, work is good for well-being if it is fairly paid, offers security and opportunities for personal development, provides space for workers to organise and express their concerns, and is non-discriminatory. In short, decent work hinges on employment that promotes workers' capabilities of life, health, voice, and so on.

In terms of paid work, there is now a range of rights established in a comprehensive body of international law aimed at promoting and safeguarding the well-being of workers. This includes such rights as a safe and healthy workplace, compensation for industrial injuries, freedom of association and to join a trade union. These rights apply to all workers irrespective of national and social origin and identity and whether they have government permission to undertake paid work. Workers' human rights are further defined through a series of ILO conventions, which elaborate and further reinforce such entitlements and call for national government laws and regulation.

Given these various social protections for workers, it might be expected that working environments would pose few threats of harm. However, we have to take account of whether countries ratify such conventions and whether they subsequently enforce them. We also have to look at ways in which laws and treaties may be circumvented in the case of undocumented and informal work. One example of such work is highlighted in the next section which draws on a film. As you read it, think about the status of the evidence offered and what it suggests in terms of the boundaries between 'harm' and 'crime'.

4.1 Looking at the evidence: statistics and 'ghosts'

The images shown in Figure 3.7 are stills from Nick Broomfield's docudrama film, *Ghosts* (2006), which offers insight into the harms a particular group of workers experienced at a particular time and place.

Figure 3.7

Still images from the film *Ghosts* depicting Chinese cockle pickers before and after the tragic drowning in Morecombe Bay

The film presents a fictional account of a real case of occupational harm – that of Chinese migrant workers who drowned whilst cockling in Morecombe Bay on the north-west English coast. The story of this real-life tragedy is recounted through the personal account of the fictionalised character Ai Qin – a young Chinese woman. The evidence supporting the making of this film is based on research, including a series of undercover investigative reports and the accounts of non-professional actors who draw on their own real-life experiences of being employed as undocumented workers in the UK. It therefore blends fact and fiction to offer powerful insights into what it feels like to be a 'hidden' worker, and the sense of powerlessness and vulnerability this engenders.

In doing so, the film suggests ways in which much of the harm experienced by Ai Qin and other undocumented workers stems from their status as 'illegal' workers. Such workers are often unaware of their rights or are reluctant to assert them, fearing that to do so may result in detainment and/or deportation. This film, then, raises questions about the causes and prevalence of the social harm involved in such incidents. Such experiences are unlikely to be reported in official statistics on occupational injury, raising questions about how far governments can and should take responsibility for controlling such work (Craig et al., 2007).

Official statistics on occupational harm, it seems, need to be treated with caution because they underestimate the extent of injuries and deaths in the workplace. Nonetheless, the statistical information that is available from the ILO does indicate that occupational injuries and deaths are a major social problem. Over 5000 people die as a result of occupational accidents or work-related diseases each day in the world. This amounts to two million deaths annually, and includes 12,000 children who die each year working in hazardous conditions. Conservative estimates suggest a further 270 million occupational accidents and 160 million cases of occupational disease each year (ILO, 2007). This suggests human wreckage, pain and suffering on an epic, global scale. The economic costs of this problem, in terms of absences from work, treatment of the sick and injured, and disability and survivor benefits, account for 4 per cent of the world's GDP – a figure twenty times greater than official development assistance to developing countries (Takala, 2002). Furthermore, the brunt of this cost is not borne by employers, but by states and the victims, many of whom are drawn from the poorest (Tombs, 2004). In 'developing' countries where the economic, social and personal impacts of occupational deaths and injuries are disproportionately concentrated, just 10 per cent or less of the workforce is likely to benefit from occupational health and safety compensation schemes. Within developed countries, where such schemes apply only to about half of the total labour force, the lowest socio-economic groups are most vulnerable to occupational death, injury or disease (Takala, 2002).

Reflecting on the different kinds of evidence presented here, it is clear that occupational injuries and deaths are a significant source of profound personal suffering and harm to the individual and wider society. On the basis of the available statistical information, many employers are clearly not exercising their legal duties to furnish healthy, safe workplaces. It would be reasonable to expect breaches of health and safety law to be reflected in crime statistics. However this is not the case. In the UK alone, only about 1000 of the approximately one million occupational injuries and deaths recorded are subject to successful criminal prosecution. Raising important questions about the relationship between the law, harm and social injustice, these features are explored below in the context of two different case studies: the first focused on the meatpacking industry, and the second involving the service sector.

4.2 Making workplaces safe? The meatpacking industry

Extract 3.3 is taken from *The Jungle,* a novel by American writer Upton Sinclair, published in 1906. It offers a fictional account of the lives of workers in 'Packingtown' – a meatpacking district of Chicago in the USA – at the beginning of the twentieth century. Like its main character, Jurgis Rudkus, many workers in the industry were immigrants. The novel explores some of the various injustices this situation produced for workers

Figure 3.8
Views of the Chicago meatpacking industry in 1900

in the meatpacking industry, controlled by a small number of powerful employers, in the absence of legislation to safeguard their rights. These injustices included: low and unpredictable wages; sexual harassment; the imposition of working hours of seventy hours or more; and the instant dismissal and 'blacklisting' of workers who engaged in trade union activity. The novel offers graphic accounts of the unsanitary and dangerous working environment in which meat was produced and the brutality to both workers and animals involved.

Activity 3.4

Take a moment to read through Extract 3.3. As you do so, think about the following questions:

■ What kind of evidence is used and what does it convey?

■ Who is responsible for the injuries described?

■ How might we conceptualise or understand the scenario it outlines as involving crime or violence?

Extract 3.3

There was another interesting set of statistics that a person might have gathered in Packingtown – those of the various afflictions of the workers. ...

... Of the butchers and floorsmen, the beef-boners and trimmers, and all those who used knives, you could scarcely find a person who has use of his thumb; time and time again the base of it had been slashed, till it was a mere lump of flesh against which the man pressed the knife to hold it. ... They would have no nails – they had worn them off pulling hides, their knuckles were swollen so that their fingers spread out like a fan. There were men who worked in the cooking rooms, in the midst of steam and sickening odours, by artificial light; in these rooms the germs of tuberculosis might live for two years ... There were the beef luggers, who carried two-hundred-pound quarters into the refrigerator-cars; a fearful kind of work ... that wore out the most powerful men in a few years. There were those who worked in the chilling rooms, and whose special disease was rheumatism; the time limit that a man could work in chilling rooms was said to be five years.

Sinclair, 2006 [1906], pp. 110–11

Comment

Although *The Jungle* is a fictional account of the working lives of employees at 'Packingtown', it was informed by the author's own research into the realities of working conditions in the meatpacking industry and was widely accepted as a realistic description of those working conditions at that time. The author initially promises statistical information in the extract, but actually provides a descriptive and visceral litany of occupational injuries suffered by workers in the animal slaughter and meatpacking industry. While this approach may be dismissed by some as partial and overly subjective, its strength is that it makes it easier for us to imagine the human suffering involved. So although statistical evidence can offer objective insights into the extent of occupational injuries and death, subjective accounts also have a role to play because they enable us to appreciate the wider social context that gives shape to such experiences and convey a sense of the associated emotions. Moreover, in the context of 'hidden' populations like undocumented workers, whose status in law often means their injuries are not officially counted, subjective accounts may well constitute the only or major source of available evidence.

Thinking back to the second and third questions regarding responsibility, crime and violence, the extract poses some dilemmas. It clearly suggests that occupational injuries were endemic in the meatpacking industry at that time; as such, it highlights the irresponsibility of employers who failed to ensure a safe work environment. Nonetheless, we may hesitate to define the physical harms described as involving violence and crime. This may be because ideas of violent crime often coalesce around 'dangerous strangers' lurking in dark places – a feature that does not pertain here. However, this fails to take account of the breadth of actions and behaviours like domestic violence and hate crimes that people experience as violent (**Fergusson and Muncie, 2008**), and suggests the need for a broader definition of crime and violence. You previously came across this idea in the context of Section 5 of Chapter 1 where it was suggested that the idea of crime may be extended to include 'social crimes' of poverty and discrimination. As regards the definition of violence, Elizabeth Stanko (2000, p. 246) defines it 'as any behaviour by an individual that intentionally threatens, attempts to inflict, or does cause physical, sexual or psychological harm to others or to her/himself'. She argues that 'violence in the context of work should not be defined solely in terms of "dangerous strangers" but should also include unacceptable conditions of work' (Stanko, 2000, p. 256). Reiman (1998) also encourages us to rethink the relationship between intention, responsibility and crime. He invites us to reflect on a scenario where an employer, aware that his workplace poses potential risks to the health of workers, does nothing to address these risks. Reiman concludes there is no moral basis for treating one-on-one harm as criminal and indirect harm as not criminal. Accordingly, the scenario outlined in Extract 3.3 could be understood as involving both criminal and violent actions on the part of employers against their employees.

Figure 3.9
Workers participating in a trade union 'Workers' Memorial Day' to protest against work-related deaths and employers' irresponsibility

The Jungle became an instant bestseller, provoking much concern about public health issues prompted by the novel's description of meat contamination and impurity. So compelling was the nature of the evidence it provided that policymakers changed the law – rapidly passing the US Pure Food and Drugs Act and the Meat Inspection Act just four months after publication of *The Jungle*. Upton Sinclair was nonetheless disappointed by the response his novel evoked: while policymakers had acted to safeguard public health, there was little response on their part to the daily injustices experienced by the workforce. As he commented: 'I aimed at the public's heart and by accident hit it in the stomach' (quoted in Schlosser, 2006, p. xi).

4.3 Labour mobilisations and the problem of regulation

In 2004, Human Rights Watch (HRW) – a non-governmental organisation (NGO) that conducts investigations into human rights abuses worldwide – revisited the terrain explored by Sinclair's novel a century earlier. It noted how, between the 1930s and 1970s, trade union activity had transformed what was still a brutal, hard and dangerous occupation into one that offered relatively secure and reasonably paid employment. However, this changed from the 1980s onwards as work processes intensified and the industry's profit motive collided with workers' rights. At the same time, the industry relocated from urban to rural settings, and in the process shed much of its unionised workforce and began to employ large numbers of migrant (especially undocumented) workers. The combination of these factors heralded a sharp decline in workers' pay and an escalation in workplace injuries, and by the beginning of the twenty-first century meatpacking had became the most dangerous factory job in the USA. The HRW report highlighted the experience of Mexican women employed as poultry workers in Arkansas. One of them told an HRW researcher how: 'In 1995 ... we did thirty-two birds a minute. I took off a year in 1998 when I had a baby. After I came back the line was forty-two birds a minute. People can't take it, always harder, harder, harder [*mas duro, mas duro, mas duro*]' (HRW, 2004, p. 36). Another worker reported that: 'The line is so fast there is no time to sharpen the knife. ... you have to cut harder. That's when it really starts to hurt, and that's when you cut yourself' (HRW, 2004, p. 35).

This case study of the meatpacking industry illustrates a number of the themes on social justice, well-being and harm that are important to this chapter. First, it reminds us that 'harm' may be physical – in this case violent. This in turn echoes Section 3 on care work, where it was noted that care receivers may be subject to violent assaults. Second, the meatpacking study raises questions about the regulation of work environments through health and safety and other laws. It shows some of the ways these laws are circumvented, and indicates how imperatives of profit and productivity may be privileged over employers' legal responsibilities to safeguard workers' life, health and bodily safety. Third, the case study emphasises the importance of taking a variety of different forms of evidence into account when thinking about harm and well-being at work – objective statistical information, fictional sources like novels, and the subjective experiences and voices of workers, many of whom are rendered even less powerful by their status in law.

4.4 Gendered work, gendered harms? Women in the service sector

Gender may influence the kinds of harm that different groups of workers are exposed to. Women, particularly those from lower socio-economic backgrounds, tend to have relatively fewer choices as to where they work, and tend to end up doing heavy, dirty, monotonous and low-paid work that increases the risks of injury, ill health and poverty (Forastieri, 2000). We shall now explore the gendered dimensions of harm using a case study taken from Barbara Ehrenreich's (2002) undercover investigation of living on the minimum wage in the USA.

Trying out the jobs for herself, in a research method known as covert participant observation, she worked as a waitress, hotel maid, house cleaner, nursing home aide, and a salesperson at Wal-Mart (a large US supermarket chain). Living in the cheapest lodgings available, she tried to live on the wages she earned. This involved long working hours and hard physical labour; to make ends meet she needed to take on at least two jobs at once. Ehrenreich's study offers insights into the physically debilitating, insecure and stressful life associated with such forms of work, and paints vivid pictures of the ways in which workers – almost all women – looked out for each other, providing mutual support and protecting their co-workers from the attention of employers in times of difficulty. This kind of support was, however, informal, since none of the jobs she took were unionised. For example, Ehrenreich recounts her first day working for a maid service:

> After a day's training I am judged fit to go out with a team, where I discover that life is nothing like the movies – at least not if the movie is *Dusting*. For one thing, compared with our actual pace, the training videos were all in slow motion. We do not walk to the cars with our buckets full of cleaning fluids and utensils in the morning, we run, and when we pull up to a house, we run with our buckets to the door. … Even dusting … gets aerobic under pressure, and after about an hour of it – reaching to get door tops, crawling along floors to wipe baseboards, standing on my bucket to attack the higher shelves – I wouldn't mind sitting down with a tall glass of water. But as soon as you complete your assigned task, you report to the team leader to be assigned to help someone else.
>
> (Ehrenreich, 2002, p. 77)

The severe harms here, like those in the meatpacking case study, were caused by various factors such as working with chemicals, continuing to work despite injury for fear of loss of pay, doing repetitive work without sufficient breaks, and so on. These physical harms are, however, largely harms of poverty and insecurity. Ehrenreich recounts the poor diet of her co-workers, their lack of health care and their struggles to make ends meet. One of these, Rosalie, lunches on half a pack of Doritos (a crisp type snack) because 'she didn't have anything in the house' and can't afford to buy lunch. Another, Maddy, a single mother, broods about her childcare problems: 'Her boyfriend's sister watches her eighteen month old for $50 per week, which is a stretch on the Maid's pay, plus she doesn't entirely trust the sister, but a real day care centre could be as much as $90 per week' (Ehrenreich, 2002, p. 80).

Ehrenreich also recounts the intensive surveillance experienced by low-paid workers – from close supervision to pre-employment personality tests and intrusive drugs testing at Wal-Mart. She goes on to recount how 'There are other, more direct ways of keeping low-wage employees in their place'; these include:

> Rules against 'gossip' or even 'talking' make it hard to air your grievances to peers or – should you be so daring – to enlist other workers in a group effort to bring about change, through a union organising drive, for example. Those who do step out of line often face little unexpected punishments, such as having their schedules or their work assignments unilaterally changed. Or you may be fired; those low wage workers who work without union contracts, which is the great majority of them, work 'at will', meaning at the will of the employer, and are subject to dismissal without explanation.
>
> (Ehrenreich, 2002, pp. 209–10)

Activity 3.5

In this section you have looked at two different case studies: one focused on the meatpacking industry, and the other involving the service sector. What do you think are the similarities and differences between the two? What precautions should we take when using the case studies as 'evidence' in drawing general conclusions about work, well-being and harm?

Comment

The most striking similarity between the case studies is the vulnerability of the workers. This vulnerability arises from a lack of legal and social protection, leaving them open to exploitation, poverty and bodily harm. This vulnerability cuts across differences between the locations, historical period and type of work. However, the differences between the case studies are significant. One is based on industrial production and one on the service sector. These differences reflect the gendering of work: at the time of the case studies, the meatpacking industry, whilst employing some female workers, was predominantly male and the service sector was predominantly female. It also tended to be easier to mobilise around struggles for workers' rights and trade union recognition in industrial settings than in fragmented, non-unionised service industries. In neither case study, though, is there much sense of well-being. However, in each of the case studies, the camaraderie arising from otherwise highly exploitative work relationships was a source of satisfaction for the workers concerned.

We can address the question of using the case studies as evidence by looking at each one in turn, asking whose voices are represented and what type of evidence is presented. It is important to note that some of the evidence in the meatpacking case study came from a report produced by a non-governmental organisation (Human Rights Watch). Given the name of this organisation, it is perhaps not surprising that it highlighted human rights abuses. While this does not detract in any way from the evidence presented, we need to be aware of the voices that are presented to us – principally those of industrial workers – and the voices of the authors of the report. In addition, the account of the US meatpacking industry presented in this section is a case study of one industry, located in a particular place, explored over a particular period of time. Looking in depth at one example enriches our analysis and helps open up important questions about how far the harm that arises in the workplace can be viewed in terms of crimes on the part of employers, and how such crimes might be regulated or controlled.

The Ehrenreich case study can be read in a similar way. The authorial voice here is that of a relatively affluent author who is investigating a subject – working conditions in the US service sector – in ways that emphasise particular themes, values and concerns. It throws a different light on the links between 'harm' and crime' compared with the meatpacking studies. The low-wage economy of service work, especially that filled mainly by part-time female labour, is more mobile and transient than the industrial or commercial forms of labour to which health and safety laws are mainly directed. The mobility and transient nature of the work means that it is also less likely to be subject to health and safety inspections which are one of the main ways in which such laws are enforced. The links between 'harm' and 'crime' are thus in a sense much weaker – harms such as low pay, long hours, intrusive surveillance and the intensification of work (also evident in the meatpacking case study) are not subject to effective external regulation, though laws governing minimum wages make some contribution to this. However, the Ehrenreich case study returns us to some of the issues raised in Section 3 on care, in particular issues of dependence and independence – here understood not only as relational dynamics (between employer and employee, and among co-workers) but also as dependence on low wages and the difficulties of developing the capabilities that might lead to a greater measure of economic independence, dignity and quality of life.

When reading these case studies we need to be cautious about how far we can use them to make general statements, for example, about harm at work, or the gendering of paid work. Other case studies might have led us to trace other forms of harm, and highlight how different kinds of harm might be experienced by different groups of workers – those in industrial versus service jobs, male or female workers, part-time or full-time work, front-line or managerial work, and so on.

Death by overtime

Japan's economy is looking healthy again - but the country's corporate warriors are not. Justin McCurry in Tokyo reports on why the salarymen are working themselves sick

Justin McCurry
The Guardian, Saturday January 13 2007

Japan's corporate warriors are victims of their own success. After more than a decade in the doldrums, Japan's economy is in the midst of its most sustained economic recovery since the bubble burst in the early 1990s. Confidence is up, but so are the demands on the salaryman's time and energy.

Japan's renaissance, far from offering its workers any respite, has them confronting a hangover from the bubble years of the 1980s: long working hours, estrangement from family and friends, ill health, and even suicide.

Millions of children still work as forced labour, says charity

Jo Revill
Sunday March 25, 2007
The Observer

On the 200th anniversary of the Slave Trade Act, a report published today highlights the fact that millions of children are still forced to work long hours for little or no money.

The charity Save The Children warns that governments, including Britain's, are not doing enough to respond to the plight of children who are trapped in conditions where they are exposed to harm, violence and extreme poverty. It calls on ministers to address the eradication of child slavery more directly by making it a central part of global poverty reduction plans.

Agenda for a fairer Britain

Labour must address taxation and its attitudes to unions if it truly wants to tackle gross inequality

John Grieve Smith
The Guardian, Friday August 31 2007

This week's revelation that the earnings of chief executives are now almost 100 times that of their average employee comes hard on the heels of a study by the Joseph Rowntree Foundation pointing to widespread dissatisfaction with the current gap between those at the top of the income scale and those at the bottom.

Slaves in Soho

Violent gangs have taken over the UK sex trade - an unacknowledged result of intervention in the Balkans.

Ros Coward
Wednesday March 26, 2003
The Guardian

If Tony Blair took a short stroll from Downing Street to Soho, the heart of London's sex trade, he'd find human rights abuses right under his nose every bit as terrible as those in Iraq. Increasingly, coercion, human trafficking and violence dominate the UK's sex industry. Yet strangely, this domestic human rights issue fails to arouse crusading zeal. Women in the sex trade, however unwillingly they arrived there, don't attract any high-minded concern.

Figure 3.10
Newspaper cuttings featuring some of the harms and hazards associated with work

5 Struggling for justice: work, welfare and the control of crime

One of the main concerns of this book is the way in which social justice is enacted (Chapter 1, Section 1). In terms of this chapter, you have seen that legal instruments such as treaties, conventions, laws and declarations do not, on their own, deliver justice. Employers, and in some cases employees, can readily find ways around them. Furthermore, while trade union pressure can be instrumental in bringing relatively greater equality to the employer/employee relationship, the curtailment of organised forms of collective pressure can render workers particularly vulnerable to a variety of different harms from intimidation, humiliation, physical injuries, and instant dismissal. For migrant workers, this vulnerability and lack of power can translate into their being excluded from the country of residence through deportation proceedings.

The HRW meatpacking case study also suggests something about the importance of a historical understanding of justice struggles. Trade union struggles between the 1930s and 1970s in the USA led to improved pay and conditions in this industry; but since then the power of workers in relation to that of employers has declined (Bluestone and Harrison, 1982). A historical perspective, then, shows that the benefits, concessions and rights that result from struggles for social justice may be fragile and contingent. They may also be quite limited, applying only to some forms of work. Thus, trade union struggles have tended to be weaker in relation to work in the female-dominated service sector than in industry, resulting in much more limited protection for workers. As Ehrenreich's study reveals, where service-based work is mobile, where workers are more transient, and where employers are themselves on the margins of economic survival, the possibility of protecting workers from harm is even more limited.

Even where laws or regulations do apply, multinational corporations can circumvent them by relocating some sorts of work overseas where fewer safeguards and protections are in place. The tendency of such corporations to violate labour rights and create dangerous conditions for workers has led many researchers to extend the meaning of crime control through a focus on corporate crime (Walters, 2008) – a theme to which Chapter 5 will return. For the moment, though, it is worth noting that such concerns have prompted some corporations to engage in activities apparently aimed at improving the well-being of workers in 'developing' countries as a demonstration of their social responsibility. Regarded by many as little more than a public relations ploy, the achievements of such initiatives are often patchy, ineffective and contradictory (Yeates, 2002). For instance, concerns about the use of child labour in developing countries to produce sporting and other consumer goods for sale in developed countries informed campaigns to exclude children from such forms of employment. This attempt to ban child labour in some cases led to a crucial loss of income for families and a shift for others into even more risky, dangerous and invisible work such as that associated with the sex trade (Jenkins et al., 2002; Kabeer, 2004). What this example suggests is a possible tension in certain social justice mobilisations between promoting the rights of vulnerable groups – workers engaged in harmful work – whilst respecting their need to safeguard their income source where there are few alternatives.

Where does this leave us in relation to certain advocacy movements' promotion of universal rights as a means of securing social justice? Here it is worth emphasising Jenkins et al.'s (2002) argument that:

> International actors [such as multinational corporations, the international labour movement] need to subordinate their notion of 'universal' labour rights to the careful appraisal of local organisations (women's groups, workers' councils, trade unions, etc.) whose strategic judgement about which issues to foreground may well determine whether the workers concerned are able to retain their jobs as well as progress their grievances.
>
> (Jenkins et al., 2002, p. 5)

That is, without fully taking into account the voices of workers themselves and the grass-roots activists who advocate on their behalf, the blanket application of universal rights may be detrimental to the workers' well-being. This reminds us of the kinds of dilemmas that rights-based approaches to social justice present, dilemmas that were explored in Chapter 1.

6   Review: work, well-being and social justice

This chapter set out to look at how well-being and harm were implicated in different forms of work. It began by identifying the shift to a focus on well-being as a feature of changing ideas, policies and practices of social welfare provision. Section 2 examined some of the implications of this in terms of how new definitions of equality focus on capabilities, sometimes at the expense of issues of distribution. Section 3 turned to care work, highlighting some of the contradictions inherent in this type of work. Here, the feminist-inspired 'ethic of care' approach, which emphasises mutuality and interdependence, was contrasted with disability activists' calls for a rights-based approach as a key plinth in struggles for independence and justice. Section 4 presented, in the form of different case studies, various types of evidence on the harms that may result from work, noting how many of these harms are not recognised or counted as crimes. Section 5 traced some of the strengths and limitations associated with certain regulatory responses addressing work-related harms.

To conclude this chapter, this section returns to the tensions between ideas of work as a source of well-being and social inclusion and work as a source of injustice and harm by revisiting the welfare-to-work policies discussed in Section 2. The various social harms associated with work explored in this chapter cast these policies in a different light, suggesting that many of those subject to such measures may be compelled to take up jobs detrimental to their well-being. Indeed, this was one of the motivations for Ehrenreich 'going undercover', as the women she worked with were precisely those subject to such welfare-to-work measures. While entry into paid work may well permit the development of new capabilities and satisfying social relationships, it may also be a major source of harm. As you saw in Section 2, welfare-to-work measures may embody a punitive dimension, becoming a means of disciplining 'problem populations' (see also Chapter 4). Peck, for example, describes how the foundation of these measures 'is to instil a basic work ethic, employment being viewed as a gradual socialisation process to which … ostensibly dysfunctional clients must be subjected if they are to achieve self-reliance (Peck, 2001, p. 175). In this account, such measures divert the excluded, disaffected and alienated away from wider social criticism or actions (such as criminal activity or 'antisocial behaviour') that threaten 'law-abiding citizens'. The promotion of paid work becomes a key strategy for managing and governing populations, a means of ensuring discipline, self-management and social stability (see Chapter 2, Section 4.3). Finally, this policy domain provides a tangible illustration of the entanglements between welfare and crime. That is, it shows how social welfare policies ostensibly concerned with promoting the capabilities, well-being and equality of some of the most vulnerable and powerless groups in society can become devices that target these groups to develop their (presumed lack of) capacity, and, in doing so, punish them for their failure to exercise their personal and social responsibility.

Further reading

If you would like to think more about some of the ideas explored here, Paddy Hillyard et al.'s *Beyond Criminology* (2004, Pluto) is a good source for the notion of social harm, while Jock Young's *The Vertigo of Late Modernity* (2007, Sage) explores the relationships between work, social inclusion, social exclusion and processes of criminalisation. Themes central to this chapter are also explored in Gerry Mooney's (ed.) *Work: Personal Lives and Social Policy* and Janet Fink's (ed.) *Care: Personal Lives and Social Policy* (both 2004, The Policy Press). Marian Barnes's *Caring and Social Justice* (2006, Palgrave Macmillan) provides a very accessible way into 'ethic of care' debates. For discussion of issues of well-being outside the global North, see Ian Gough and J. Allister McGregor's (eds) *Wellbeing in Developing Countries* (2007, Cambridge University Press).

References

Barnes, M. (2006) *Caring and Social Justice*, Basingstoke, Palgrave Macmillan.

Beechey, V. (1986) 'Studies of women's employment' in Feminist Review (ed.) *Waged Work: A Reader*, London, Virago.

Bluestone, B. and Harrison, B. (1982) *The Deindustrialisation of America*, New York, NY, Basic Books.

Cochrane, A. and Talbot, D. (eds) (2008) *Security: Welfare, Crime and Society*, Maidenhead, Open University Press/Milton Keynes, The Open University.

Craig, G., Gaus, A., Wilkinson, M., Skrivankova, K. and McQuade, A. (2007) *Contemporary Slavery in the UK: Overview and Key Issues*, York, Joseph Rowntree Foundation.

Department for Communities and Local Government (DCLG) (2007) *Fairness and Freedom: The Final Report of the Equalities Review*, London, DCLG; also available online at http://archive.cabinetoffice.gov.uk/equalitiesreview/publications.html (Accessed 8 January 2008).

Ehrenreich, B. (2002) *Nickel and Dimed: On (Not) Getting By in America*, New York, NY, Owl Books.

Fergusson, R. and Muncie, J. (2008) 'Criminalising conduct?' in Cochrane, A. and Talbot, D. (eds) (2008) *Security: Welfare, Crime and Society*, Maidenhead, Open University Press/Milton Keynes, The Open University.

Forastieri, V. (2000) 'Information note on women workers and gender issues on occupational health and safety', Programme on Safety and Health at Work and the Environment (SAFEWORK), Geneva, ILO; also available online at http://www.ilo.org/public/english/protection/safework/gender/womenwk.htm (Accessed 26 November 2007).

Fraser, N. (1995a) *Justice Interruptus: Critical Reflections on the 'Postsocialist' Condition*, London, Routledge.

Fraser, N. (1995b) 'From redistribution to recognition? Dilemmas of justice in a "post-socialist" age', *New Left Review*, I/212, July–August, pp. 68–93.

Ghosts, film, directed by Nick Broomfield. UK: Nick Broomfield, 2006.

Heron, E. and Dwyer, P. (1999) 'Doing the right thing: Labour's attempt to forge a new welfare deal between the individual and the state', *Social Policy and Administration*, vol. 33, no. 1, pp. 91–101.

Hillyard, P., Pantazis, C., Tombs, S. and Gordon, D. (eds) (2004) *Beyond Criminology: Taking Harm Seriously*, London, Pluto.

Hoggett, P. (2000) *Emotional Life and the Politics of Welfare*, Basingstoke, Macmillan.

Human Rights Watch (HRW) (2004) *Blood, Sweat and Fear*, New York, NY, Human Rights Watch; also available online at http://www.hrw.org/reports/2005/usa0105/usa0105.pdf (Accessed 26 November 2007).

International Labour Organization (ILO) (2007) *The ILO at a Glance*, Geneva, ILO; also available online at http://www.ilo.org/global/About_the_ILO/lang–en/docName–WCMS_082367/index.htm (Accessed 9 January 2008).

Jenkins, R., Pearson, R. and Seyfang, G. (eds) (2002) *Corporate Responsibility and Labour Rights*, London, Earthscan.

Jordan, B. (2006) *Social Policy for the 21st Century*, Cambridge, Polity Press.

Kabeer, N. (2004) 'Globalization, labor standards, and women's rights: dilemmas of collective (in)action in an interdependent world', *Feminist Economics*, vol. 10, no. 1, pp. 3–35.

Lewis, J. (2001) 'Legitimising care work and the issue of gender equality' in Daly, M. (ed.) *Care Work: The Quest for Security*, Geneva, ILO.

Mooney, G. and Neal, S. (eds) (2009) *Community: Welfare, Crime and Society*, Maidenhead, Open University Press/Milton Keynes, The Open University.

Nussbaum, M.C. (2006) *Frontiers of Justice*, London, Belknap Press.

Nussbaum, M.C. and Sen, A.K. (eds) (1993) *The Quality of Life*, Oxford, Clarendon Press.

Peck, J. (2001) *Workfare States*, New York, NY, The Guilford Press.

Pollert, A. (1981) *Girls, Wives, Factory Lives*, London, Macmillan.

Reiman, J.H. (1998) *The Rich Get Richer, The Poor Get Poorer: Ideology, Class and Criminal Justice* (5th edn), Boston, MA, and London, Allen & Bacon.

Schlosser, E. (2006) 'Foreword' in Sinclair (2006).

Sen, A.K. (1999) *Development as Freedom*, Oxford, Oxford University Press.

Sevenhuijsen, S. (1998) *Citizenship and the Ethics of Care: Feminist Considerations on Justice, Morality and Politics*, London, Routledge.

Sinclair, U. (2006 [1906]) *The Jungle*, Harmondsworth, Penguin.

Stanko, E. (2000) 'Rethinking violence, rethinking social policy' in Lewis, G., Gewirtz, S. and Clarke, J. (eds) *Rethinking Social Policy*, London, Sage Publications/ Milton Keynes, The Open University.

Takala, J. (2002) 'Introductory report: decent work – safe work', paper presented at XVIth World Congress on Safety and Health at Work, Vienna 26–31 May, Geneva, ILO.

Tombs, S. (2004) 'Workplace injury and death: social harm and the illusions of law' in Hillyard, P., Pantazis, C, Tombs, S. and Gordon, D. (eds) *Beyond Criminology: Taking Harm Seriously*, London, Pluto.

Tronto, J. (1993) *Moral Boundaries: A Political Argument for an Ethic of Care*, New York and London, Routledge.

Twigg, J. (2000) *Bathing: The Body and Community Care*, London, Routledge.

Walters, R. (2008) *Eco Crime and Genetically Modified Food*, London, Routledge.

World Health Organization (WHO) (2002) *Missing Voices*, Geneva, WHO.

Yeates, N. (2002) 'Globalization and social policy: from global neoliberal hegemony to global political pluralism', *Global Social Policy*, vol. 2, no. 1, pp. 69–91.

Young, I.M. (1990) *Justice and the Politics of Difference*, Princeton, NJ, Princeton University Press.

Chapter 4
'Problem' populations, 'problem' places

Gerry Mooney

Contents

1   Introduction

Previous chapters argued that social justice as an idea and an ideal is interwoven with issues of inequality, poverty and social exclusion. It is a comparatively straightforward task in the era of World Wide Web access (though by no means everywhere or for everyone) to locate sources of information illustrating the extent of poverty and inequality, though much of the latter, particularly in relation to the ownership and distribution of wealth, or, as Chapter 3 showed, undocumented labour or unpaid care, remains considerably under-researched or 'hidden'. While we may seek to take some comfort from assumptions that discussions of poverty and inequality should start from questions of social justice, this contrasts with long-standing ideas that the poor are a 'problem', at times a 'dangerous' population. Such populations are also often associated with particular places; for instance, with ghettos, deprived estates and slums. Hence the title of this chapter, '"Problem" populations, "problem" places'.

As you saw in Chapters 2 and 3, it is important to understand that how poverty and inequality are perceived and how poor people are labelled say much about the policies that are likely to be developed in response. Viewing poor and disadvantaged groups as a 'vulnerable' section of society requiring social welfare and other forms of state support stands in sharp contrast to those representations of the poor as an 'undeserving' group, and to arguments that there is an 'underclass' of impoverished and 'disorderly' people, cut-off from the rest of society. In practice, as you will see as the discussion unfolds, such distinctions are rarely as clear-cut as this terminology implies. Furthermore, notions of disadvantaged or excluded groups as a 'problem population' do not arise in a vacuum but mirror the wider social relations of inequality. They carry with them particular associations of social class, 'race' and gender and ideas about how social life should be organised. As Chapter 2 also emphasised, poverty is often viewed as a deficiency in the way that poor people conduct their family and personal lives, in their attitudes to work, and so on. Through such arguments poverty comes to be understood not as an outcome of the society in which we live, a product of state failure or of an inadequate welfare state, but as a consequence of 'negative' or 'dysfunctional' attitudes, behaviours and ways of life that necessitate control. People living in poverty may be those who are viewed as not having developed their capabilities. This takes us back to the key questions on social justice/injustice raised in Chapter 1, in particular to that which relates to the intersections between social welfare and crime control strategies.

While images of the feckless poor have been with us for a long time, since the 1980s there has been a marked shift in political attitudes towards poverty both in the UK and more widely. These tend to represent poverty, disadvantage and exclusion in terms of poor people contributing to their own precarious socio-economic situation. Examining some of the different forms that approaches to poverty take in different parts of the world allows us to draw out the important commonalities between them.

The aims of this chapter are to:

■ Explore some of the many complex and different ways in which questions of social justice and of inequality come to be seen in terms of the deficient behaviour of different problem populations. In particular, it explores how particular groups of people and particular places come to be identified as 'problem populations' and how social welfare and crime concerns intersect in the management of these populations.

■ Highlight some of the enduring legacies of the past, both in terms of the language that is often mobilised to represent disadvantaged and poor people, and also the continuing presentation of certain groups as 'problems' to be managed. While highlighting some of these historical legacies, this chapter also draws attention to the 'newer' ways in which the notion of problem populations is being mobilised.

As you read the chapter, you are encouraged to reflect on some of the possible historical antecedents that might influence contemporary manifestations of such ways of thinking, as well as on how ideas of problem populations come to be associated with particular social groups and geographical places. You might also wish to reflect on why it is that the idea of problem populations is rarely, if ever, associated with rich and powerful groups.

Like Section 4 of Chapter 3, this chapter is structured around a series of case studies. Through a range of case studies from the USA, France and Britain it explores some manifestations of the representation of poor people as problem populations in different national contexts in the early twenty-first century. Before proceeding to explore these it is important to consider the role of a case study in work such as this. Case studies offer what we might term 'windows' on particular events which allow wider themes and processes to be revealed. In concentrating light on an issue, case studies allow us to make comparisons and enable bigger claims to be made. In this chapter, a case study approach is used to illuminate ideas of problem populations and problem places. Case studies are valuable tools to help us make sense of a particular issue, but we must also be sensitive to their limitations. The choice of case studies reflects the particular values and perspectives of the person making the selection. We need to be alert to the subject matter of the study, reflecting on what is the focus, which voices are being heard (or are missing), and from what perspective claims are being made. The case studies in this chapter involve selected extracts, comments from eyewitnesses, media sources, politicians, political commentators and social scientists; they also include photographs and other images. As you work with these you need to pay attention to what is being claimed – and what might be missing from the arguments advanced. We shall return to these issues during the chapter, and in Chapter 6 you will revisit wider questions around the selection and choice of evidence.

2   New Orleans and Hurricane Katrina: 'shaming America'?

I begin our story with a case study relating to one of the most momentous episodes of environmental catastrophe in the early 2000s, Hurricane Katrina. On 29 August 2005, Katrina, a category 5 hurricane with 290 kph winds, hit the Gulf of Mexico coast of the southern USA, bearing down on the state of Louisiana and in particular on its main city, New Orleans (Figure 4.1). With much of 'the Big Easy', as the city is popularly known in the USA, below sea level, New Orleans was protected from the sea, a surrounding lake and the Mississippi River by a ring of natural and human-made barriers called levees. However, Katrina was the long-awaited and feared 'Big One', a powerful storm with the potential to overwhelm the levees. When the storm struck, a number of critically important levees gave way and, in scenes that were soon to be broadcast around the world, more than 80 per cent of New Orleans was inundated with several feet of toxic floodwater (Figure 4.2). The majority of the population of 1.3 million in the greater New Orleans area had already been evacuated in what was the largest forced migration in recent US history, but those remaining, primarily in areas home to predominantly black and working-class people and with large numbers of elderly people and children, were quickly engulfed by the floodwater. To date, at least 1000 people are known to have died, while the final death figure may never be known. The estimated costs of damage range from US$100bn to US$200bn (Gotham, 2007, p. 81).

Katrina's impact on New Orleans was one of the most televised disasters in recent history, generating twenty-four-hour news coverage around the world and considerable political debate. The response to the disaster by the US Federal Government in Washington DC and organisations such as the Federal Emergency Management Agency (FEMA) was criticised for being insufficiently quick and effective. In the ensuing controversies in the aftermath of Katrina, however, the government was not the only target of critics. Hurricane Katrina was widely perceived as the largest 'natural' disaster to occur in continental USA. However, for many

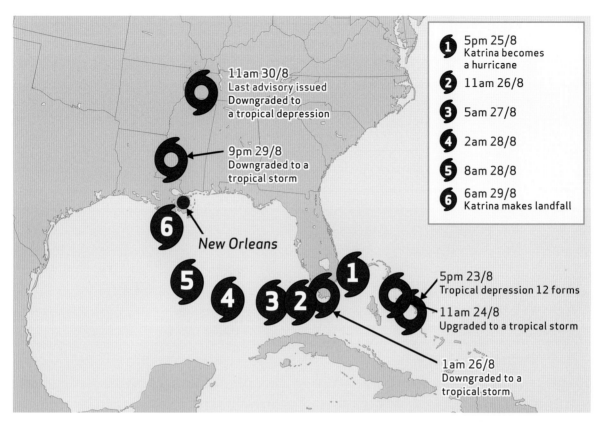

1 5pm 25/8
Katrina becomes
a hurricane

2 11am 26/8

3 5am 27/8

4 2am 28/8

5 8am 28/8

6 6am 29/8
Katrina makes landfall

11am 30/8
Last advisory issued
Downgraded to
a tropical depression

9pm 29/8
Downgraded to a
tropical storm

6

New Orleans

5 4 6 3 2 6 1

5pm 23/8
Tropical depression 12 forms

11am 24/8
Upgraded to a tropical storm

1am 26/8
Downgraded to a
tropical storm

All times EDT (Eastern Daylight Time)

observers this was no natural disaster but an unprecedented social disaster. Highlighting reports of looting, rape, murder and street violence, some conservative commentators claimed that social organisation broke down into some kind of 'anarchy'. These accounts were often repeated uncritically on the television, accompanied by sensationalised and selective film coverage. Such stories and images, together with political indifference and initial government failure to respond to the disaster, amounted to what *The Economist* termed 'The shaming of America' (*The Economist*, 10 September 2005, p. 11).

The conservative focus on, and allegations of, widespread crime and social disorder were contradicted by other eyewitness accounts. In the extract that follows, two white paramedics from San Francisco talk about their experiences in trying to escape from the flooding in New Orleans across a bridge connecting the mainly black New Orleans City to the largely white suburbs of Jefferson Parish.

Figure 4.1
The path of Hurricane Katrina, 25 August to 30 August 2005

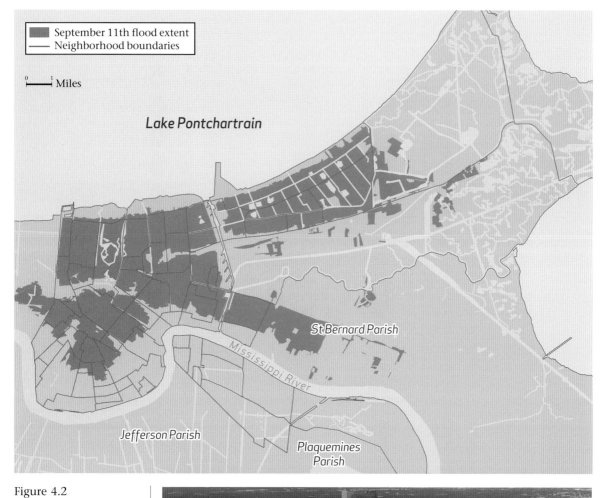

Figure 4.2
Map showing extent
of flooding in New
Orleans, 11 September
2005; flood waters in
New Orleans, 30 August
2005

Extract 4.1

As we entered the center of the city, we finally encountered the National Guard. The guard members told us we wouldn't be allowed into the Superdome [a sports arena], as the city's primary shelter had descended into a humanitarian and health hellhole. They further told us that the city's only other shelter – the convention center – was also descending into chaos and squalor, and that the police weren't allowing anyone else in.

Quite naturally, we asked, 'If we can't go to the only two shelters in the city, what was our alternative?' The guards told us that this was our problem – and no, they didn't have extra water to give to us. This would be the start of our numerous encounters with callous and hostile 'law enforcement.'

We walked to the police command center at Harrah's on Canal Street and were told the same thing – that we were on our own ... We held a mass meeting to decide a course of action. We agreed to camp outside the police command post. We would be plainly visible to the media and constitute a highly visible embarrassment to city officials. The police told us that we couldn't stay. Regardless, we began to settle in and set up camp.

In short order, the police commander came across the street to address our group. He told us he had a solution: we should walk to the Pontchartrain Expressway and cross the greater New Orleans Bridge to the south side of the Mississippi, where the police had buses lined up to take us out of the city.

The crowd cheered and began to move. We called everyone back and explained to the commander that there had been lots of misinformation ... The commander turned to the crowd and stated emphatically, 'I swear to you that the buses are there.'

We organized ourselves, and the 200 of us set off for the bridge with great excitement and hope. As we marched past the convention center, many locals saw our determined and optimistic group ...

Families immediately grabbed their few belongings, and quickly, our numbers doubled and then doubled again. Babies in strollers now joined us, as did people using crutches, elderly clasping walkers and other people in wheelchairs. We marched the two to three miles to the freeway and up the steep incline to the bridge. ...

As we approached the bridge, armed sheriffs formed a line across the foot of the bridge. Before we were close enough to speak, they began firing their weapons over our heads. This sent the crowd fleeing in various directions.

As the crowd scattered and dissipated, a few of us inched forward and managed to engage some of the sheriffs in conversation. ... The sheriffs informed us that there were no buses waiting. The commander had lied to us to get us to move.

We questioned why we couldn't cross the bridge anyway, especially as there was little traffic on the six-lane highway. They responded that the West Bank was not going to become New Orleans, and there would be no Superdomes in their city. These were code words for: if you are poor and Black, you are not crossing the Mississippi River, and you are not getting out of New Orleans.

...

All day long, we saw other families, individuals and groups make the same trip up the incline in an attempt to cross the bridge, only to be turned away – some chased away with gunfire, others simply told no, others verbally berated and humiliated. Thousands of New Orleaners were prevented and prohibited from self-evacuating the city on foot.

Bradshaw and Slonsky, 2005, pp. 4, 5

What emerges from this account is the sharp collision in the aftermath of the hurricane between the rapidly increasing welfare needs of an already largely impoverished population and the predominant concerns of the police and other government agencies with crime prevention and controlling the population affected by flooding (Figure 4.3). The sense of injustice felt by people fleeing the floods, with few personal belongings and in urgent need of food, fresh water and shelter, was compounded by the response of the police which was primarily concerned with preventing this largely black, working-class and poor population from entering the more affluent and 'whiter' suburbs around New Orleans. However, it would be mistaken to suggest that crime was not a real issue, even though we need to be aware of the sensationalised reportage of much of it. The floods did give rise to looting and to other criminal behaviour, but one might reflect that some forms of these could be interpreted as desperate attempts to find food, water and shelter in appalling conditions. In some respects, the aftermath of Katrina and the story offered here provide yet another example of how poverty, 'disorderly' behaviour and criminal activity come to be seen as closely interlinked. There are other important issues highlighted in this account. One of these is the failure of the state to provide for the afflicted sections of the New Orleans population. Another is the organised response from the people themselves. Contrary to representations of poor people as 'passive' and 'idle', many of those most adversely affected by Katrina were not prepared, or were unable, to sit

out the disaster until the government chose to respond. Instead, they mobilised collectively to find safety and protest against the injustices they suffered.

In terms of evidence, Bradshaw and Slonsky (2005) offer an important eyewitness report highlighting some of the growing social tensions in New Orleans following Katrina. This kind of report not only provides alternative sources of evidence to that available in the mainstream media, it also provides rich insights from which we can develop greater understanding of the impacts of disasters such as hurricanes on different groups of people. Such eyewitness accounts offer some sense of the immediacy of the disaster, as well as how this impacted on the personal lives of those concerned, in ways that official government reports and statistics are often unable to deliver. They also show that there are different, often contradictory, stories and interpretations of events in the aftermath of the flooding. Through these we can begin to get some idea

Figure 4.3
Images of armed police on patrol in New Orleans contrast sharply with other images showing victims of the floods struggling to cope with the devastation wrought by Katrina

of the political controversies that Katrina sparked. These conflicting accounts were also played out on the web-based alternative media and in television documentaries. One such television documentary was *When the Levees Broke*. Produced in 2006 by the African American political film director Spike Lee, this documentary focused on the experiences of poor black people in New Orleans. Television footage and films of the kind produced by Lee show us not only the availability of other forms of evidence of the impacts of the Katrina disaster but also how such accounts are contested. *When the Levees Broke* generated controversy for its damning portrayal of the Bush Government and its attack on sensationalised and selective stories about crime during the aftermath of the disaster.

The disaster has also generated critical commentary from social science researchers on key aspects of contemporary US society that some would prefer to remain hidden from view. These include the gross social inequalities that are to be found across urban America, as well as the failures of government policy before, during and after Katrina to meet the most basic requirements of many millions of American citizens (see SSRC, 2007). It touched a raw nerve around questions of 'race' and class, inequalities between rich and poor, the role of government, and global climate change. In the words of *New York Times* journalist David Brooks, hurricanes such as Katrina 'wash away the surface of society, the settled way things have been done. They expose the underlying power structures, the injustices, the patterns of corruption and the unacknowledged inequalities' (September 2005, quoted in Strolovitch et al., 2005, p. 1). In these respects, the disaster illustrates wider issues of social inequality, discrimination, marginalisation and poverty. Katrina provided an opportunity for long-standing US-wide political controversies to be re-energised, and within days of the disaster different interpretations of its underlying causes, who or what was to blame, and what was required to rebuild New Orleans were resounding in the media and in political debates (Peck, 2006).

Activity 4.1

Below are four extracts from different commentators reflecting on the impact of Hurricane Katrina on New Orleans. In what ways do they offer contrasting interpretations of the events? What are the key competing themes that emerge from these quotations? And how might these understandings shape potential government responses?

Extract 4.2

Katrina didn't turn innocent citizens into desperate criminals. This week's looters (not those who took small supplies of food and water for sustenance, but those who have trashed, burned, and shot their way through the city since Monday) are the same depraved individuals who have pushed New Orleans' murder rate to several multiples above the national average in normal times. ... Today may not be the best day to get into New Orleans' intractable crime problem, but it's necessary, since it explains how this week's communications and policing vacuum so quickly created a perfect storm for the vicious lawlessness that has broken out. ...

...

... Now no civil authorities can re-assert order in New Orleans. The city must be forcefully demilitarized, even as innocent victims literally starve.

Gelinas, 2005

Extract 4.3

The chaos after Hurricane Katrina did not cause a civilizational collapse; it simply exposed and magnified one that had already occurred ... A strange admixture of upper-class decadence and underclass pathology, New Orleans has long been a stew of disorder and dysfunction, convincing many New Orleans residents, years before Hurricane Katrina, to evacuate what they regarded as an increasingly unlivable city ... The squalor and crime in the Superdome represented nothing more than the squalor and crime transferred from New Orleans' legendary hellish housing complexes [and the] countless images of stranded women, children and the elderly were explained far more by the absence of fathers than the tardiness of FEMA [Federal Emergency Management Agency].

Neumayr, 2005, pp. 48, 50

Extract 4.4

In the confusion and suffering of Katrina ... most white politicians and media pundits have chosen to see only the demons of their prejudices. The city's complex history and social geography have been reduced to a cartoon of a vast slum inhabited by an alternately criminal or helpless underclass, whose salvation is the kindness of strangers in other, whiter cities. Inconvenient realities ... have not been allowed to interfere with the belief, embraced by New Democrats as well as old Republicans, that black urban culture is inherently pathological.

Davis, 2006a

Extract 4.5

It is difficult, so soon on the heels of such an unnecessarily deadly disaster, to be discompassionate, but it is important in the heat of the moment to put social science to work as a counterweight to official attempts to relegate Katrina to the historical dustbin of inevitable 'natural' disasters. ...

... [T]he supposed 'naturalness' of disasters here becomes an ideological camouflage for the social (and therefore preventable) dimensions of such disasters, covering for quite specific social interests. Vulnerability, in turn, is highly differentiated; some people are much more vulnerable than others. Put bluntly, in many climates rich people tend to take the higher ground leaving to the poor and working class land more vulnerable to flooding and environmental pestilence. ... In New Orleans ... topographic gradients doubled as class and race gradients, and as the Katrina evacuation so tragically demonstrated, the better off had cars to get out. ... [T]heir immediate families likely had resources to support their evacuation, and the wealthier also had the insurance policies for rebuilding. ...

...

... The race and class dimensions of who escaped and who was victimized by this decidedly unnatural disaster not only could have been predicted, and was, but it follows a long history of like experiences. ... In New Orleans there are already murmurings of Katrina as 'Hurricane Bush.' It is not only in the so-called Third World, we can now see, that one's chances of surviving a disaster are more than anything dependent on one's race, ethnicity and social class.

Smith, 2006

Comment

There is a shared emphasis across each of the extracts above that Katrina was a 'social' as opposed to a 'natural' disaster. But there are sharply differing perspectives on offer between the first and second quotations, on the one hand, and the third and fourth ones on the other, as to what this might mean and how it is to be interpreted. There is no appeal to any shared 'evidence' to adjudicate over this. Gelinas and Neumayr reflect conservative 'blame-the-victim' stereotypes of the social problems that characterise US cities today (Macek, 2006). In addition, there is an implicit anti-urbanism here which reproduces long-held views of cities as places of deprivation and depravity, of social disorganisation and criminality. There is also a view, most notable perhaps in the Neumayr reference to public housing ('New Orleans' legendary hellish housing complexes'), that state policy and what passes as state welfare in the USA has contributed to 'the problem'. This is captured most notably by the reference to an 'underclass', a concept which, as developed and utilised in the US context, is frequently used as shorthand for poor urban blacks and black pathology (Young, 2007).

The idea that poor people are responsible for their own situation is reflected in US government policy which, since the 1980s in particular, has dismantled public welfare programmes and reduced expenditure on the kinds of public services that were so badly needed following Katrina. The language and sentiments that pervade the quotations from Gelinas and Neumayr focus on the behaviour and deficits of the poor in New Orleans, which are seen as symptomatic of a wider 'malaise' across US society. By contrast, Davis and Smith locate Katrina within the wider social fabric of US society: they point to the ways in which inequalities come to shape the landscape of cities such as New Orleans – in particular, the racial and class segregation that characterises the districts in which different groups of people live. This unequal social geography, characteristic of many of the world's cities today, contributes to the marked differences in the experiences of socio-economic security and insecurity on the part of different groups of the population (**Cochrane and Talbot, 2008a**). Here, the US government is accused of abandoning the poor of New Orleans at a time of critical need, a claim that chimes with other criticisms of the Bush Administration for failing to address the sense of vulnerability and injustice felt by many poor people across urban America:

> The Katrina disaster revealed the stark politics that surround 'security' in post 9/11 United States. A dark irony emerges here. On the one hand, a large proportion of Bush's rhetoric since 9/11 has emphasised the fragile exposure of US urbanites to purported 'terrorist' risks. ... On the other hand, US cities' preparedness for much more devastating and likely impacts of catastrophic 'natural' events such as Katrina have actually been undermined because of fiscal cuts and the construction of the vast 'homeland security' and anti-terror drive which tends to ignore or downplay such risks.
>
> (Graham, 2006)

The concern to control the New Orleans poor is evidenced by the activities of the police and by the militarisation of the city in the days that followed the hurricane. For critics, the real crime of Katrina, however, was the failure of the state to respond quickly and effectively to the needs of the most vulnerable, protect from harm, and provide for the environmental security of those parts of the city and populations threatened by flooding (which had been forecast for many years previously). In Section 5 of Chapter 1 and in Chapter 3, the idea of social harm was introduced. By using this notion to reflect on the claims above that Katrina was no 'natural' disaster, we can develop our understanding of the ways in which the unequal social geography of New Orleans, the failure to offer adequate protection from storms and hurricanes, and the activities of the various law enforcement agencies all contributed to the vulnerability and insecurity experienced by many of the city's poorest groups. This is a much broader appreciation of the 'crimes' of Katrina than those often portrayed and helps us to further comprehend the complex interrelationship between crime, social harm and welfare.

3   Worlds apart? The problem of problem places

Katrina offers us a rich case study through which we have begun to explore some of the concerns of this chapter. In reflecting on the controversies that emerged in the aftermath of Katrina, we can see that for some commentators it was a 'problem place' long before the hurricane struck in 2005. The idea that different places can be seen as problematic is a recurring theme that emerges in the context of ongoing debates around poverty and inequality, and the relationship between social justice and criminal justice across the world. In particular, urban spaces have often been viewed as sites of problem populations.

Activity 4.2

In the extract below, French sociologist Loïc Wacquant offers us some ways of understanding the idea of problem places. What do you feel are the main themes that are raised by this commentary? And how might we reflect on the different sources of attention that these localities receive and to which he refers?

Extract 4.6

Ghetto in the United States, *banlieue* in France, *quartieri periferici* (or *degradati*) in Italy, *problemområde* in Sweden, *favela* in Brazil, *villa miseria* in Argentina, *rancho* in Venezuela: the societies of North America, Western Europe, and South America all have at their disposal in their topographic lexicon a special term for designating those stigmatized neighbourhoods situated at the very bottom of the hierarchical system of places that compose the metropolis. It is in these districts draped in a sulfurous aura, where social problems gather and fester, that the urban outcasts of the turn of the century reside, which earns them the disproportionate and disproportionately negative attention of the media, politicians, and state managers. They are known, to outsider and insiders alike, as the 'lawless zones', the 'problem estates', the 'no-go' areas or the 'wild districts' of the city, territories of deprivation and dereliction to be feared, fled from, and shunned because they are – or such is their reputation ... – hotbeds of violence, vice and social dissolution.

Wacquant, 2008, p. 1

Comment

It is immediately striking that each different national context has a vocabulary carrying a pejorative rhetoric which produces and sustains the notion of problem places. The social and the geographical come together in notions such as 'the problem estate' to describe particular places – and also their populations – as being characterised by social problems and as locales of crime and disorder. These localities are often symbolic, representing all that is problematic about urban life and society more broadly. They become catchwords for a diverse assortment of social ills and work to identify these social ills as belonging to particular places and their inhabitants. In other words, while Wacquant himself identifies ghettos and other problem areas as part of a wider system of social stratification and inequality that characterises the urban world today, this is not a prevailing view. Disadvantaged locales are more generally understood as the *sources* of urban (and wider) social problems. This is reflected across a range of urban social policies and regeneration programmes that speak of 'poor people and poor places' and carry ideas about what they *should be like*. In other words, a sharp distinction is drawn in the language identified by Wacquant between 'normal' and 'deviant' ways of living. It is the culture that exists in poor places, rather than the wider social organisation, which is constructed as being the obstacle to the successful eradication of poverty, crime and other social problems. This recourse to cultural explanations of poverty is encapsulated in the terms 'culture of poverty' (Lewis, 1966) and 'cycle of deprivation' (Joseph, 1972). Through these terms, two worlds are created: the world of 'mainstream' or 'normal' society ('us') on the one hand, and the world of the needy, the deviant and the criminal ('them') on the other. As you saw in Chapter 2, this binary division informs and permeates understandings of social exclusion and inclusion, an issue to which we shall return in the Review section of this chapter. Wacquant highlights the kind of language used by politicians, policymakers and the media to describe problem places, and it is important that we be aware of the sources of such language, why it is being used, by whom and for what purpose. It is equally important to note that alternative images and accounts, generated by the residents of places so labelled, are often neglected.

Following the discussion around some of the controversies surrounding the aftermath of Hurricane Katrina, the main concern of this section is to explore some of the other ways in which populations in need or in danger come to be seen as a problem for wider society. Here the emphasis is on how they come to be seen as a problem associated with *particular places*. In other words, the focus is on how *types of people* inhabiting *types of places* come to be problematised. There are many different ways in which these problematisation processes have emerged historically – from the fears of politicians and of the rich of the slum-dwellers and crime-ridden 'rookeries' of nineteenth-century London, the closes and wynds of Glasgow, the 'little Irelands' of Manchester and other British cities, through to the concerns of politicians with 'problem estates' in the 1980s and 1990s. As noted previously in this chapter, the creation of particular places as problems, places of danger and crime, and places in and of need is common to different countries. But across these different national contexts, they take on particular meanings and understandings. To illustrate this point, the next two subsections focus on two such places: the suburban housing estates of urban France (the '*banlieue*'); and the council estate in parts of the UK.

3.1 Urban unrest: the case of the French urban periphery

'France had a rebellion of its underclass', argued American social scientist Immanuel Wallerstein (2005). He was referring to the 'unrest' or 'riots' which began on Thursday 28 October 2005 in Clichy-sous-Bois, a large public housing estate, or *banlieue*, on the outskirts of Paris, and then spread to a number of other areas across urban France. The riots were sparked by the accidental deaths of two young boys fleeing the police. The boys were subsequently referred to by the then Interior Minister (and later French President) Nicolas Sarkozy as 'delinquent scum' (quoted in Ossman and Terrio, 2006, p. 6). Nearly 300 neighbourhoods across France were affected by the ensuing unrest; within the space of three weeks, around 10,000 vehicles had been destroyed and almost £200m damage done to property. Sarkozy's response was to declare a state of emergency and demand a series of severe penal sanctions against those involved in the unrest. Such a response was symptomatic of deep-seated antipathy towards, and growing fear of, the criminality and disorder associated with places such as Clichy-sous-Bois experienced by some sections of French society. But his subsequent order in November that all 'foreigners' found guilty of rioting were to be deported, whether they were in France legally or not, not only fuelled further resentment but also highlighted many of the underlying tensions in French society.

The term *banlieue* does not translate easily into English. *Banlieues* are generally suburban districts around the major French cities, but they do not equate with suburbs as the term is generally used in the UK. As French Marxist philosopher Etienne Balibar notes:

> There are *banlieues* and *banlieues*, often geographically very close to one another but separated by a social abyss and a permanent antagonism ...: some are rich, even very rich ...; others are symbols of poverty, the decline of public services, the relegation of ethnic minorities and poor whites, unemployment and stigmatization ... In many respects, even if the riots extended to other urban areas (especially outside Paris), it was this clash *within the banlieue*, between the two worlds it contains, that was characteristic. ... *the banlieue ... is a frontier, a border-area and a frontline.*
>
> (Balibar, 2007, p. 48)

The worlds that Balibar highlights are shaped by patterns of migration, France's colonial past and present, and its class structure. According to one commentator, a line is increasingly drawn in French society 'between the Français-de-souche (white-Catholic-French) and those of color, primarily "new" immigrants from North and sub-Saharan Africa' (Orlando, 2003, p. 395), many of whom are Muslim, impoverished and live in *banlieue* neighbourhoods. Large-scale development of the *banlieue* began in the 1960s, resettling both working-class populations moving from inner-city areas and migrants arriving from various French colonies. The construction of what were often high-rise, public-sector housing estates accompanied the relocation of manufacturing industries and the expansion of new industrial areas in the suburbs. As in the UK, such estates reflected political and policymaking concerns to provide better housing predominantly for the white working-class population but in the process also created new patterns of social segregation.

Figure 4.4

Wreckage of two cars in a market in Clichy-sous-Bois, Paris, following riots in October 2005; and youths rioting in Clichy-sous-Bois, 28 and 29 October 2005

By the 1990s, the *banlieue* had become a byword for a range of social ills: industrial decline; rising poverty; urban decay; high unemployment; declining public services; and a rapidly deteriorating physical environment. Increasingly used to house black and Arab populations, the French mainstream media and political elites also associated them with poverty, criminality and social decay. They were a world removed from 'traditional' (i.e. white Catholic) French society, a world in which social tensions between disaffected youth and the police regularly spilled over into unrest. For some commentators, as well as for many residents in the *banlieue*, the unrest in late 2005 was a rebellion against police harassment, poverty and the racism of French society. For Wallerstein (2005) it also reflects the growing social polarisation accompanying the steady urbanisation of the world's population. Ossman and Terrio (2006) also draw out the wider global processes that are at work here, commenting:

> If the French riots of 2005 so dominated international news, it is not simply due to Americans' desire to punish the French for their position on Iraq, or plays of one upmanship on the part of the British. It is that they are an occasion to explore a reconceptualization of the spaces of danger, culture, territory, and sovereignty that is taking place. Since the 1980s car burnings, supermarket lootings, and

destruction of police stations in projects outside Paris, Lyon, and Strasbourg have been discussed not only as a time bomb ticking in the suburbs, but as an intifada [uprising] of the suburbs perpetrated by ghetto hoodlums. ... [I]t is only too apparent that the backdrop for such discussions of the events in France was an image of a vague, transnational suburban zone that each national government is engaged with containing and controlling on its own territory.

(Ossman and Terrio, 2006, p. 14)

Here, the global echoes of unrest in France can be seen in the ways that it brings together issues around war, migration, security and injustice (see also **Cochrane and Talbot, 2008b**). In the early twenty-first century, such issues take on a renewed vigour amidst the rising levels of inequality and the growing tensions between the global rich and poor, not only played out in developing countries but also in the centres of global capitalism, such as in the UK, France and the USA. And the use of the term 'intifada', while pointing to specific Palestinian revolts against Israeli occupation, also speaks to the increasing perception in the Judaeo-Christian West of the 'threat' posed by Islam.

Our brief journey around the events in France in late 2005 suggests many issues about the identification of disadvantaged groups as problem populations. From the example of the *banlieue* we can also see that, over time, particular places come to accommodate populations, such as working-class slum-dwellers or other marginalised populations such as immigrants, which are seen as being vulnerable and in need in some way. This is the reconceptualisation of problem people and problem places to which Ossman and Terrio (2006) refer in their reflection on continuity and change in the construction of particular locales as dangerous places of social decay and violence.

Activity 4.3

Reflecting on the case studies of New Orleans (Section 2) and the *banlieue* in this section, how do wider social inequalities and social divisions shape the experiences of the populations in these localities? What would you identify as the shared themes that emerge in these case studies?

Comment

As in New Orleans, 'race' and class come together in the French urban periphery in particular ways. The marginalised populations in each are the product of migrations which, though reflecting different colonial pasts, share a present as the internally excluded in their respective national contexts. Both populations are seen as dangerous yet vulnerable due to high rates of unemployment, poor housing and entrenched economic insecurity. There are also common themes about the failures of state welfare and the social impacts of reductions in welfare spending. Issues of crime and disorder are also brought into focus: we can see how such issues came to be the dominant concerns of governments and local agencies. In both contexts, sections of the mainstream media and politicians mobilised pre-existing racist antipathies to reproduce stereotypes of the populations of both locales as criminal and disorderly. Against this, the marginalised populations of the French *banlieue* and New Orleans struggle to draw attention to issues of poverty, racism, the erosion of welfare, and police hostility – in other words, to a range of social harms and crimes of the state. The hurricane in New Orleans and oppressive policing in the *banlieue* were merely the sparks that reignited the fires of social injustice.

3.2 Bringing it all back home: the 'problem estate'

It would be mistaken to deduce from the discussion thus far that problem populations and problem places only occur elsewhere. The focus of this section is to consider how such understandings also emerge in the UK. Our case study here is formed around a specific type of place which in recent decades has increasingly come to be perceived as a 'problem' – the deprived council estate.

Activity 4.4

In *Estates: An Intimate History* (2007), Lynsey Hanley offers an autobiographical account of being raised in a suburban council estate in Birmingham in the 1960s and 1970s. Read the following short extract from Hanley's story and think about the following questions. What do these tell us about how council estates might be perceived in the UK today? And what, if any, criticisms would you make of her claims?

Extract 4.7

The Wood. I was born there, and lived there between the ages of eighteen months and eighteen years. Even though I have lived away from home for over a third of my life now, it continues to shape the way I think about the world outside it. ... [I]t's a lifelong state of mind.

...

It's not something you think about when you're growing up. *Wow, I'm really alienated. My school is suffering from its single-class intake.* ... It's more a sense you have. A sense that someone, who lives in a proper house, in a proper town, sat on the floor of an office one day with a box of fancy Lego bricks and laid out ... a way of housing as many people as possible in as small a space as could be got away with. And, in so doing, forgot that real people aren't inanimate yellow shapes with permanent smiles ... That real people might get lost in such a place.

I wonder if the stigma of coming from a council estate is ever turned to an advantage, and whether that inherent sense of inferiority ever becomes a source of pride. You believe yourself to be proud of having overcome the limitations of your environment – literally, of having escaped a kind of prison – and yet you know that in some ways you will never escape. That's because, to anybody who doesn't live on one (and to some who do), the term 'council estate' means hell on earth.

Council estates are nothing to be scared of, unless you are frightened of inequality. They are a physical reminder that we live in a society that divides people up according to how much money they have to spend on shelter. My heart sags every time it senses the approach of those flat, numbing boxes that prickle the edges of every British town.

Hanley, 2007, pp. 4, 5

Comment

Hanley provides a vivid description of what is often referred to as 'council estate living'. The gloomy image that is offered, however, is not out of step with the dominant representations of estates that circulate today. Elsewhere in her book we are invited to play word association with the term 'council estate', and Hanley provides some assistance by listing 'alcoholism, drug addiction, relentless petty stupidity, a kind of stir-craziness induced by chronic poverty and the human mind caged by the rigid bars of class' (2007, p. 7). But we could go much further than this by adding youth offending, teenage pregnancies, unemployment, welfare and benefit 'cultures', violence and disorder. Hanley's account fits well with wider mainstream media representations of estates which use these locales and their populations in crime dramas and documentary programmes built around CCTV footage. In addition, there are the representations carried in the print and electronic media that speak of neighbours and estates 'from hell', that tell us which are Britain's 'worst' estates and towns, and which generally make strong connections between council estates and some of the worst forms of youth offending. For example, in Scotland a close association is made between 'neds' (generally interpreted as non-educated delinquents) and council estates (**Fergusson and Muncie, 2008**). Council estates have also featured as convenient backdrops of social disorganisation in popular fiction and journalism, in travelogues, and as a source of political commentary and policy debate. In the late 1990s and early 2000s, for instance, it was the council estate which was marked out by the New Labour Government as one of the key locales of 'social exclusion' in British society.

Hanley sees estates as a symbol of failure for everyone but particularly for those who live in them. Estate life forms a 'wall in the head' (Hanley, 2007, pp. 148–9), a particular state of mind producing a distinctive set of aspirations. These social psychological claims strongly parallel ideas that council estates generate their own subcultures that signal such places as different from others. This is also replicated by some journalists:

> The truth is that council housing is a living tomb. You dare not give the house up because you might never get another, but staying is to be trapped in a ghetto of both place and mind. ... The people in them need to have better training and more incentives to work. And council estates need to be less cut off from the rest of the economy and society.
>
> ...
>
> ... It is not British civilisation that ails ... It is British council estates. ... We made them. Now we need to unmake them, doing whatever it takes.
>
> (Hutton, 2007)

The context of Will Hutton's assertions was a debate sparked by a series of murders of teenagers in estates in South London in early 2007. In making the generalisation that council estates are ghettos, like Hanley he underestimates the degree of heterogeneity and internal social differentiation that exists *within* estates. Communities are very rarely undifferentiated in the way that either Hanley or Hutton implies (**Mooney and Neal, 2009**) and the suggestion that there is something approaching a ghetto or estate mentality reproduces stigmatising stereotypes of particular social groups, including among them some of the most deprived sections of society.

Council estates did not always carry the social stigma that is attached to them now. In the 1920s and 1930s and for a considerable time after the Second World War they met the acute housing needs of millions of people across the UK. It is important therefore that we historicise the idea of the 'problem estate'. To help with this, let us consider briefly some important research conducted by sociologist Seán Damer in Glasgow in the 1970s and 1980s. Damer's concerns lay with the history of a particular council estate in the Govan district of Glasgow. Constructed between 1934 and 1935 as one of the city's many 'rehousing' estates (or 'schemes'), the Moorepark scheme accommodated some of the families displaced through slum-clearance programmes. By

Figure 4.5
Council housing was much in demand in the 1950s and 1960s as suggested by this photograph of the post-war new town of Hemel Hempstead, published in the photographic news magazine *Picture Post* in 1954. Such images belie the later image of many council estates as 'problem' places

the 1970s, the estate had come to achieve local and Glasgow-wide notoriety as an alleged locale of violence, drunkenness and assorted other social problems, and it was increasingly referred to by what became its better-known label, 'Wine Alley' (Damer, 1989).

The label 'Wine Alley' says much about the negative reputation attached to Moorepark. On the basis of interviews with tenants, housing and council officials, and police officers among others, and using detailed examination of archival records and reports produced by Glasgow Corporation and relevant Scottish Office departments from the 1930s, Damer was able to demonstrate how ideas of a 'problem family', 'problem tenant' and 'problem estate' first developed in the 1930s and not only came to apply to the residents of Moorepark but (especially in the post-1945 era) became more widespread as ways of representing particular sections of the council housing population.

Damer's detailed research sought to locate the factors that would explain why this reputation had developed, and his work is important not least for the ways in which it illuminates the historical evolution of the ideas of problem people and problem places. Through this research he

Figure 4.6

Moorepark housing scheme, Glasgow, early 1970s. This was typical of Glasgow's 1930s' 'slum-clearance' estates

reminds us that contemporary negative representations are not recent developments but in significant ways are contemporary manifestations of historical processes. However, we need to be alert to some of the potential problems that can emerge in using historical evidence to develop the kinds of argument with which we are concerned in this chapter. It is important to avoid interpreting the rationales and meanings of policies from the past from the perspective of contemporary debates and arguments. One of the ways in which Damer avoids such a pitfall is by considering how the discourses of problem tenants and places came to be reinvented in the 1960s and 1970s (see also Johnstone and Mooney, 2007).

There is the further problem of what might be termed 'hindsight', the tendency to see past events as the unfolding of one story whereas there may be competing and conflicting stories. And we may only be able to generate partial understandings from the available historical evidence base. Not only is incomplete evidence open to different interpretations, but evidence can be selectively used depending on the larger story that the author wishes to convey or the argument being advanced. In attempting to frame historical evidence in terms of contemporary concerns and arguments, we need to allow for the possibility of other stories, meanings and understandings. However, properly located in the context of wider social and political developments at the time in question, historical evidence is invaluable in helping us understand some of the enduring legacies of the past that pervade images and representations of 'problem' people and places today.

In relation to the themes of this chapter, historical research helps us to uncover the continuities between the perceptions of problem places in Victorian Britain, notably the slums and rookeries of the late nineteenth-century city, the emergence of 'problem estates' in the post-1945 period, and more contemporary terms such as 'sink' estates, 'hard-to-let' estates, 'inner-city' and *banlieue*. While the historical circumstances which produced these neighbourhoods, and the terms generated to signify them, are different, there is a striking similarity in the purpose of the latter. These terms separate out the inhabitants of these 'problem' places from the 'mainstream' or 'normal' society – and ritually degrade, humiliate and blame them for their poverty and deprivation in the process. We also need to be alert to the international appeal and spread of the idea of problem places. Ideas and representations of problem places are not confined to European and North American contexts: they are also manifested in the 'favelas', 'barrios' and 'ghettos' that characterise many 'Third World' cities (Davis, 2006b; Neuwirth, 2006). The idea of the 'Third World slum' is explored further in Chapter 5.

Given that such segregation and stigmatisation are central components of so many societies across the world, we may conclude that the idea of populations of problem places as somehow marginal to society is a myth. This 'myth of marginality' (Perlman, 1976) both presents people living in poverty as hopeless, deficient and disorganised masses surplus to society, and obscures the complex interrelations between different forms of economic activity. Stigmatisation of the kind highlighted in the work of Damer and others devalues the experiences, perspectives and voices of people who live in places regarded as problematic. People who live in *banlieue* estates, slums, shanty towns and disadvantaged council estates are still people, struggling to build their lives and to survive. In such localities a myriad of resourceful coping and 'getting-by' personal, household and community strategies emerge in an effort to 'keep going'. Thus, people develop their skills and capabilities (Chapter 3) in struggling to make ends meet in a context where the economic resources available to them are deficient. Coping strategies represent but one dimension, albeit an important one, of the ways in which poor people struggle to make better lives. Other strategies that demonstrate the presence of capacities are political struggles – be they for better resources, welfare support or community facilities – and resistance against stigmatisation and negative labelling. As **Pinkney and Saraga (2009)** highlight in relation to campaigns to defend community services in the early twentieth century, and as others have explored in previous time periods (Lavalette and Mooney, 2000; Fox-Piven and Cloward, 1977), disadvantaged people have a long tradition of collective organisation and mobilisation to 'get heard' (Burnett, 2006).

4   Review: misrecognition, disrespect and the politics of fear

A recurring theme in discussions of poverty is the distinction between 'the poor' and 'the non-poor'. Echoing nineteenth-century ideas of the 'deserving' and 'undeserving' poor, or 1930s notions of 'problem estates', such distinctions continue to permeate representations of poor populations today and also often figure prominently in policy.

Table 4.1 Constructing worlds apart: 'us' and 'them'

'Us'	'Them'
Society at large	The underclass
Employment	The workless
Independence/self-help	Dependency
Stable family	Single mothers
Law-abiding	The criminal
Orderly	Disorderly
Natives	Immigrants
Victims	Criminals
Respectable	Disreputable
Included	Excluded

Source: adapted from Young, 2007, p. 22

Binary classifications such as those highlighted in Table 4.1 have long underpinned the ways in which poor and disadvantaged populations are seen as distinctive from 'the rest of society'. In this way we can talk of the poor being 'Other'. 'Othering' (Lister, 2004, pp. 100–101; Young, 2007, pp. 5–7) refers to the categorisations of the poor and other populations – for example, some migrant groups (though not others) and single parents – as variously undeserving and deficient. Othering works to present such groups as distinct, different from 'normal society'; it underpins how the non-poor, and many politicians, policymakers and sections of the mainstream media, think and talk about, and act towards, poor people (see also Chapter 2, Section 3). In this way, 'the underclass', for instance, is constructed as a distinct and generally homogeneous group, even if no robust evidence has been produced that an underclass actually exists. One particular link that we can draw between the poor areas of New Orleans, *banlieues* and council estates is that they are generally portrayed as homogeneous localities inhabited by deficient people. The case studies highlight the importance of particular imaginations of places and people; problems are defined, diagnosed and policies developed and targeted at them to 'cure' them.

Such processes both reflect and reproduce the kinds of discrimination and social injustices highlighted in Chapter 1 that blame people living in poverty for their own situation and for society's problems. People living in poverty may be demonised but they are also feared; feared for who they are – or who they are thought to be – and resented for representing a state of existence into which others fear to fall. History also reminds us that the fear of sudden descent into cataclysmic long-term poverty, with its inevitable terminus in the dreaded workhouse, was the nightmare of the British working class until the Second World War and the subsequent development of the welfare state.

As we have seen, poor and other disadvantaged populations tend to experience not only a lack of material resources but also a lack of respect. This returns us to important questions of social (in)justice. Chapters 1 and 3 introduced arguments made by Iris Marion Young (1990) that, alongside questions of access to resources, we need to consider how people are recognised and valued.

Activity 4.5

Reflecting on the discussion of recognition and respect in Section 5 of Chapter 1, in what ways do the representations of disadvantaged populations and places, as considered in the case studies in this chapter, reflect issues of 'non-recognition' and 'disrespect'? How might these be reflected in policy outcomes?

Comment

'Non-recognition' and 'disrespect', which involve being rendered either invisible or routinely maligned and stigmatised in everyday vocabularies and through policymaking, is the lived experienced of disadvantaged groups. This social devaluation is an important dimension of social injustice and it compounds inequalities of material resources. It infringes human and citizenship rights, denying voice and agency to those who are treated in this manner. In some ways, as we have seen in all our examples, the problem of problem populations can be that they have 'too much' voice and agency, especially when they are resisting, rebelling, and struggling for social justice – but of the 'wrong sort'! But non-recognition and disrespect work in other ways too, shaping social and crime control policies. Viewing the problems experienced by poor people as the problems *of* poor people leads to a focus on their lifestyles and behaviours of the kind that we met in Chapter 2. Ideas of social inclusion and exclusion, therefore, reflect the translation of material disadvantages and need into cultural processes. In turn, the redistributive dimensions of social justice argued for by Fraser (1995) and others (e.g. Levitas, 2005; Lister, 2004) are rejected as viable policy options. Misrecognition and disrespect provide what we might see as a 'triple whammy' – stigmatising the poor, pathologising welfare and material need, and obscuring the inequalities of wealth and income.

This chapter has explored some of the many ways in which poor and disadvantaged groups come to be regarded as problem populations afflicted by assorted deficiencies. It has highlighted how these processes can be understood as part of a generalised war, not on poverty, inequality or injustice, but on poor people themselves (Gans, 1995). In each of the case studies that featured in this chapter, the different populations can be seen as vulnerable to environmental disasters, reductions in (or the absence of) welfare, state hostility and apathy, and to the denial of voice, agency and respect. At the same time, they are also often seen as an actual or potential threat to society. The coming together of particular class-based and assumed racial characteristics with an assortment of ascribed cultural and social deficiencies enables such populations to be represented as being both in need and ever more disorderly and threatening – an enemy 'within'. In this way, problem populations come to be target populations, whose ways of living and whose cultures that enable survival are under attack.

While poor and problem populations are often constructed as marginal or surplus to society, they play a central role in the dominant debates about poverty and inequality that circulate in the world today. As Perlman (1976) and Stallybrass and White (1986) have forcefully argued, that which is marginal is usually symbolically central. Problems of social injustice and the unequal social relations of poverty, wealth and inequality become pitched as the cultural deficiencies of the poor, necessitating intervention in efforts to 'develop' cultures and personal lives and behaviour. Here, we can see also the collisions between welfare and crime control: how what are 'crimes' of acute, unmet welfare needs come to be portrayed as behaviours and cultures requiring control and management.

This brings us back to the central idea of this book: social justice. We can see that economic disadvantages and cultural disrespect are interrelated in important ways. Poor people are resented, scapegoated, stereotyped, 'viewed through a social lens which renders most of their existence invisible while focusing on every blemish and dysfunction of their existence' (Young, 2007, p. 75). By contrast, the behaviour, lifestyles and cultures of the rich and powerful have received comparatively little attention. Rarely are these social groups seen as a problem population. Nor are the rapidly spreading gated communities and enclaves that many rich people inhabit seen as problem places. What this implies is that the lens of our investigation and analysis should not approach poverty in isolation from wealth, nor the poor in isolation from the rich, but should see them both as part of a wider social whole characterised by pervasive and entrenched social inequalities.

Further reading

For further discussion and explanations of events in New Orleans in the aftermath of Hurricane Katrina, G. Squires and C. Hartman's (eds) *There is No Such Thing as a Natural Disaster* (2006, Routledge) brings together a series of social sciences essays and commentaries around different dimensions of the disaster. There are many books and studies detailing the evolution of council estates in Britain and focusing on the many problems facing some of the residents who live in them. Tony Parker's *People of Providence: A Housing Estate and Some of Its Inhabitants* (1983, Hutchinson) is widely recognised as a pioneering study of life in a council estate. Providing extracts from detailed interviews with residents, it highlights the diverse lives and ordinary and extraordinary stories which characterise life in these neighbourhoods. David Kynaston's *Austerity Britain, 1945–51* (2007, Bloomsbury) offers a rich and accessible historical overview of a key period in post-war Britain, including accounts of life in some of the new council estates being built during this time. In *Social Exclusion* (2005, Open University Press), David Byrne examines the origins of terms such as 'underclass' and 'exclusion' and considers some of the ways in which these are replicated in social and geographical divisions in contemporary British society. For representations of social disorganisation and council estates in works of fiction, see Livi Michael's *Under a Thin Moon* (1994, Minerva) and Andrea Levy's *Never Far From Nowhere* (1996, Headline Review).

References

Balibar, E. (2007) 'Uprisings in the *Banlieues*', *Constellations*, vol. 14, no. 1, pp. 47–71.

Bradshaw, L. and Slonsky, L.B. (2005) 'The real heroes and sheroes of New Orleans', *Socialist Worker* (US, 9 September; also available online at http://www.socialistworker.org/2005-2/556/556_04_RealHeroes.shtml (Accessed 11 July 2007).

Burnett, L. (2006) *'Dignity Shouldn't Have to Be Earned!' Get Heard Scotland: Final Report*, Glasgow, The Poverty Alliance.

Cochrane, A. and Talbot, D. (eds) (2008a) *Security: Welfare, Crime and Society*, Maidenhead, Open University Press/Milton Keynes, The Open University.

Cochrane, A. and Talbot, D. (2008b) 'War, disease and human security' in Cochrane and Talbot (eds) (2008a).

Damer, S. (1989) *From Moorepark to 'Wine Alley'*, Edinburgh, Edinburgh University Press.

Davis, M. (2006a) 'Who is killing New Orleans?', *The Nation*, 10 April; also available online at http://www.thenation.com/doc/20060410/davis (Accessed 25 January 2007).

Davis, M. (2006b) *Planet of Slums*, London, Verso.

The Economist (2005) 'The shaming of America', *The Economist*, vol. 376, issue 8443, 10 September, p. 11.

Fergusson, R. and Muncie, J. (2008) 'Criminalising conduct' in Cochrane and Talbot (eds) (2008a).

Fox-Piven, F. and Cloward, R.A. (1977) *Poor People's Movements: Why They Succeed and How they Fail*, New York, NY, Pantheon Books.

Fraser, N. (1995) 'From redistribution to recognition? Dilemmas of justice in a post-socialist age', *New Left Review*, vol. 212, July–August, pp. 68–93.

Gans, H. (1995) *The War Against the Poor*, New York, NY, Basic Books.

Gelinas, N. (2005) 'A perfect storm of lawlessness', *City Journal*, 1 September; also available online at http://www.city-journal.org/printable.php?id=1867 (Accessed 14 January 2007).

Gotham, S.F. (2007) 'Critical theory and Katrina: disaster, spectacle and immanent critique', *City*, vol. 11, no. 1, pp. 81–99.

Graham, S. (2006) 'Cities under siege: Katrina and the politics of metropolitan America' [online], 11 June; available at 'Understanding Katrina: perspectives from the social sciences' [SSRC online forum], http://understandingkatrina.ssrc.org/Graham/ (Accessed 3 May 2007).

Hanley, L. (2007) *Estates: An Intimate History*, London, Granta.

Hutton, W. (2007) 'Open the gates and free people from Britain's ghettos', *The Observer*, 18 February; also available online at http://observer.guardian.co.uk/comment/story/0,,2015638,00.html (Accessed 8 February 2008).

Johnstone, C. and Mooney, G. (2007) '"Problem" people, "problem" places? New Labour and council estates' in Atkinson, R. and Helms, G. (eds) *Securing An Urban Renaissance*, Bristol, The Policy Press.

Joseph, K. (1972) 'The cycle of deprivation', speech to the Conference of Pre-School Playgroups Association, 29 February, reprinted in Joseph, K. *Caring for People*, London, Conservative Political Centre.

Lavalette, M. and Mooney, G. (eds) (2000) *Class Struggle and Social Welfare*, London, Routledge.

Levitas, R. (2005) *The Inclusive Society* (2nd edn), London, Palgrave Macmillan.

Lewis, O. (1966) *La Vida*, New York, NY, Random House.

Lister, R. (2004) *Poverty*, Cambridge, Polity Press.

Macek, S. (2006) *Urban Nightmares*, Minneapolis, MN, University of Minnesota Press.

Mooney, G. and Neal, S. (eds) (2009) *Community: Welfare, Crime and Society*, Maidenhead, Open University Press/Milton Keynes, The Open University.

Neumayr, G. (2005) 'The desolate city', *The American Spectator*, November, pp. 48–50.

Neuwirth, R. (2006) *Shadow Cities*, London, Routledge.

Orlando, V. (2003) 'From rap to rai in the mixing bowl: beur hip-hop culture and banlieue cinema in urban France', *Journal of Popular Culture*, vol. 36, no. 3, pp. 395–415.

Ossman, S. and Terrio, S. (2006) 'The French riots: questioning spaces of surveillance and sovereignty', *International Migration*, vol. 44, no. 2, pp. 5–21.

Peck, J. (2006) 'Neoliberal hurricane: who framed New Orleans?' in Panitch, L. and Leys, C. (eds) *Coming to Terms with Nature: Socialist Register 2007*, London, Merlin Press.

Perlman, J. (1976) *The Myth of Marginality*, Berkeley, CA, University of California Press.

Pinkney, S. and Saraga, E. (2009) 'Communities and mobilisation' in Mooney, G. and Neal, S. (eds) *Community: Welfare, Crime and Society*, Maidenhead, Open University Press/Milton Keynes, The Open University.

Smith, N. (2006) 'There's no such thing as a natural disaster' [online], 11 June; available at 'Understanding Katrina: perspectives from the social sciences' [SSRC online forum], http://understandingkatrina.ssrc.org/Smith/ (Accessed 9 June 2007).

Social Science Research Council (SSRC) (2007) 'Understanding Katrina: perspectives from the social sciences' [online forum], http://understandingkatrina.ssrc.org/ (Accessed 12 November 2007).

Stallybrass, P. and White, A. (1986) *The Politics and Poetics of Transgression*, London, Methuen.

Strolovitch, D.Z., Warren, D.T. and Frymer, P. (2005) 'Katrina's political roots and divisions: race, class and federalism in American politics' [online], 11 June; available at 'Understanding Katrina: perspectives from the social sciences' [SSRC online forum], http://understandingkatrina.ssrc.org/FrymerStrolovitchWarren/ (Accessed 11 January 2007).

Wacquant, L. (2008) *Urban Outcasts: A Comparative Sociology of Advanced Marginality*, Cambridge, Polity Press.

Wallerstein, I. (2005) 'The inequalities that blazed in France will soon scorch the world', *The Guardian*, 3 December; also available online at http://www.guardian.co.uk/comment/story/0,,1656654,00.html (Accessed 8 January 2008).

When the Levees Broke: A Requiem in Four Acts, television documentary, directed by Spike Lee. USA: HBO Documentary Films, 2006.

Young, I.M. (1990) *Justice and the Politics of Difference*, Princeton, NJ, Princeton University Press.

Young, J. (2007) *The Vertigo of Late Modernity*, London, Sage.

Chapter 5
The globalisation of social justice

Allan Cochrane and Reece Walters

Contents

1   Introduction

In Chapter 2, John Clarke indicated how the national framing of equality, justice and welfare questions has been challenged by globalist conceptions of, and struggles for, social justice. This chapter takes up this problematic more fully, exploring the difference that adding the prefix 'global' makes to the ways we think about social justice.

The aims of this chapter are to:

■ explore some ways in which a global perspective illuminates the entanglements between social welfare and crime control

■ examine how 'thinking globally' impacts upon questions of social order, social change and social policy in the contemporary world.

The chapter revisits some of the issues and concepts introduced earlier in the book, particularly in Chapter 1, by placing them in a global context. We live in a world where the rhetorics of peace, equality and fairness surround our daily existence; yet the meanings attached to such values are not universally shared and are often contested. In the process of shifting the focus in this way, a further aim of the chapter is to:

■ show how different forms of evidence can be used to make sense of these issues, both to understand how forms of inequality and injustice are constituted and to consider some of the ways in which they might be challenged. It focuses in particular on ways of interpreting and understanding familiar sorts of evidence, considering how evidence is collected by journalists as they develop newspaper and magazine articles. It asks what the difference between academic and journalistic evidence might be.

We begin by looking at what 'thinking globally' might mean.

Activity 5.1

What does the word 'global' mean to you? How relevant is a global understanding of the world to the way you live your life?

Comment

For most of us the 'global' probably conjures up notions of the world as shared space, perhaps best summed up in the image of the Earth viewed from outer space (as in Figure 5.1(*top*)). From that perspective the globe is a more or less unified object on whose surface the boundaries between nations – and indeed the nations themselves – are not apparent. Such a vision might be contrasted to one of the world as an international space (as in Figure 5.1(*bottom*)). This vision of the global sees the world as made

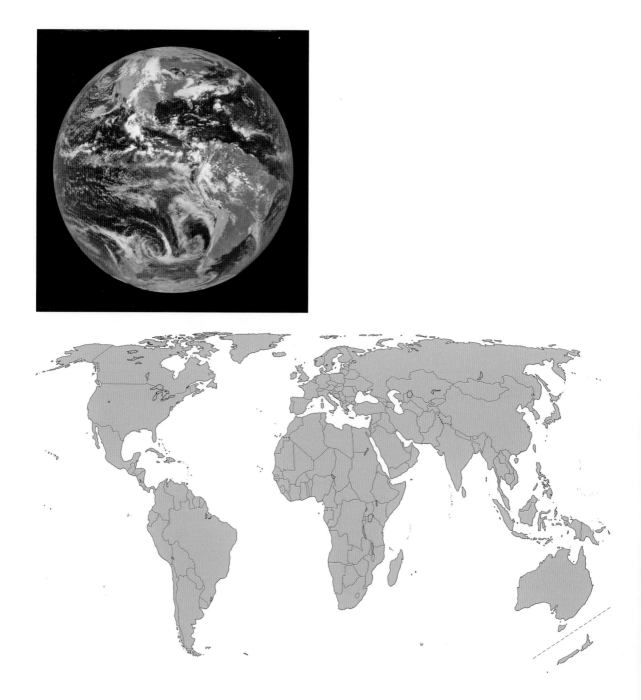

Figure 5.1
Earth viewed from
outer space; global
political geography

up of a series of countries – spaces demarcated by political borders and identities. Although the terms 'global' and 'international' are often used interchangeably, an understanding of the world as global has rather different implications from an understanding of the world as international.

How you respond to the first question in Activity 5.1 might also influence your answer to the second. If you start from a more globalised understanding of the world, that might encourage you to focus on shared challenges facing humanity as a whole. You might therefore be concerned about the threats to the future existence of humanity and the ecosystems supporting us that are posed by climate change. You might also be concerned about forms of social inequality around the world, and about the ways in which poverty seems predominantly to be concentrated amongst certain populations wherever they live. Such a global understanding might influence you to join campaigns against global poverty and for global justice. The Live 8 concert and the Make Poverty History campaign in 2005, with all their tensions and contradictions, are instances of attempts to raise awareness of global inequities and mobilise resources to combat them.

Thinking globally also reminds us of the ways in which markets around the world are connected through globe-spanning networks of production, distribution, sales, consumption and recycling. Recognising how the production and consumption of various goods and services are embedded in geographically dispersed networks encourages us to think about how the ways in which we live our lives connect us to the lives of other people in other parts of the world. It also enables us to see connections between seemingly disparate areas of policy, trade and consumption – and of the entanglements of social welfare and crime control.

Activity 5.2

Next time you shop at your local supermarket, count the items in your trolley from different countries. How many countries are represented in your weekly shopping? What sort of impacts do you think your visit to the supermarket has on people living thousands of miles away?

Comment

The availability of food varieties from near and far, which provides supermarket shoppers with delicious out-of-season foods, comes with environmental and social costs. For example, the pollution created from long-distance transportation, the erosion of soils, the sale of contaminated meat, the illegal use of chemicals, the exploitation of farm workers, the use of fraudulent marketing practices, and the aggressive trade policies of governments and corporations may all be part of the process that gives us 'consumer choice'.

The focus of this chapter is the environment, in terms of both human settlements and the social and ecological systems that support them. In Section 2, we consider slums as one kind of human settlement which is of increasing importance given that more people are living in urban areas. Here we highlight the emergence of a 'global' social policy in the form of responses by international organisations such as the United Nations and World Bank to the rise of the urban slums, and consider its 'local' application. Traditionally, slums have been defined as places within which 'dangerous' or 'problem' populations are clustered (see Chapter 4), and attempts have been made either to get rid of these problem people (e.g. through slum clearance) or to manage them (often harshly). However, such approaches have increasingly been challenged by other ones which seek to redefine slums and people living in them as sources of hope and innovation.

Section 3 turns to explore the challenges that relate to common resources (e.g. air, water and natural habitat) and the ways in which they are managed. This idea of common resources can be viewed as another way of approaching the question of 'the social basis of social justice' introduced in Chapter 1; but here 'the social' relates to a common humanity that transcends specific populations and societies bounded by national borders. Our focus on common resources highlights the extent to which the management of these resources is underpinned by structures of power and inequality. These structures mean that some populations are left relatively powerless and marginalised while others benefit. This focus also indicates the extent to which these processes may have negative consequences, even for those they seem to benefit; for example, providing greater consumer choice may degrade the environment in ways that impact adversely on the beneficiaries. Section 3 also explores the extent to which it may be valid to interpret some of the actions of the powerful not only as harmful but also as criminal.

Section 4 goes on to consider what sorts of responses might be appropriate to meet these global challenges. In other words, it examines some of the implications of 'globalising' social justice. This is considered through a brief discussion of transnational judicial or legal frameworks relating to environmental injustice. Section 5 draws the arguments of the chapter together.

2 Urbanisation and the challenge of the global slums

Urbanisation is a global phenomenon: the world is becoming increasingly urbanised, with more than half of the population now living in urban areas. As Gerry Mooney showed in Chapter 4, it is no longer possible – if it ever was – to divide the world into a 'developed' world with big cities, and an 'underdeveloped', 'peasant' or 'Third' world, without cities. Certainly some areas of the world (North America,

Figure 5.2
Urbanisation and the
global slum

Europe, Japan) are more heavily urbanised than others, but there is no neat line that can be drawn on the globe to divide a world of urbanites from a world of peasants. In fact, the fastest growing urban areas are in the poor countries of the world, not the rich ones.

The process of urbanisation has been accompanied by a massive expansion in places identified as 'slums'. Slums are defined by the United Nations as 'characterised by overcrowding, poor or informal housing, inadequate access to safe water and sanitation, and insecurity of tenure' (Davis, 2006, pp. 22–3). According to a report prepared by UN-HABITAT (the United Nations Human Settlements Programme), '[o]ne out of every three city dwellers – nearly one billion people – lives in a slum' (2006, p. 11).The rise of the slum has become a powerful symbol of the lived realities of millions of people and of contemporary global divisions. These realities are expressed in films, documentaries, photographic imagery and popular journalism, from street children to overcrowding, violence and shanty towns. These often represent slums as dysfunctional and threatening, yet also vibrant and dynamic.

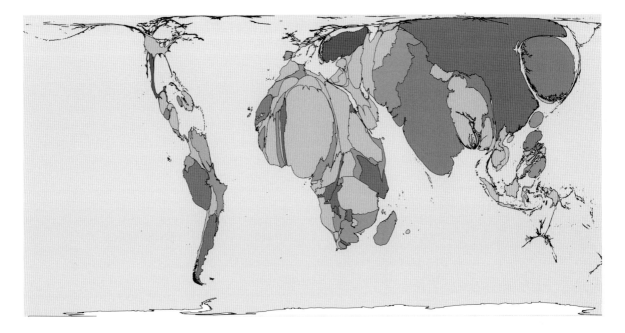

There is little argument about the growth of the slums: they are now recognised as a key aspect of contemporary urban life. This is illustrated by Figure 5.3, which shows the growth in the numbers of people living in urban slums in different parts of the world between 1990 and 2001. Poorer territories have experienced greater slum growth than richer territories – but the number of people living in slums has increased in 85 per cent of territories from 1990 to 2001. Slums are a global phenomenon, not only because they are increasing around the world but also because they are fundamental expressions of global processes of social change – reflecting the emergence of new divisions alongside the maintenance of older ones. Castells (1998) has tried to capture this in his notion of the 'Fourth World' which he identifies as a 'new geography of social exclusion'. He argues that:

> It is formed of American inner-city ghettoes, Spanish enclaves of mass youth unemployment, French banlieues warehousing North Africans, Japanese Yoseba quarters and Asian mega-cities' shanty towns. And it is populated by millions of homeless, incarcerated, prostituted, criminalized, brutalized, stigmatized, sick, and illiterate persons.
>
> (Castells, 1998, pp. 164–5)

Figure 5.3
On this world map, each territory has been resized according to the proportion of all extra people to start living in slums between 1990 and 2001 who live in that territory. The map shows how rates of slum growth vary between continents. It is also possible to identify differences between regions

2.1 Urbanisation: harbinger of development and equality?

In the past, a distinction was often made between 'modern' urbanised societies and 'backward' peasant societies. In the former the expectation was that old social divisions are broken down, encouraging greater equality and higher levels of household income across society, while in the latter it was assumed that people are trapped within their existing class and caste positions. To what extent are such distinctions helpful in the context of the rise of the global slums?

Instead of urbanisation being a harbinger of 'modern' development, as the optimists might have hoped, in this 'planet of slums' (Davis, 2006) it seems to reinforce social inequality. As UN-HABITAT notes:

> Large sections of the population in urban areas are suffering from extreme levels of deprivation that are often even more debilitating than those experienced by the rural poor, to the extent that urban poverty is becoming as severe and dehumanizing as rural poverty.
>
> (UN-HABITAT, 2006, p. ix)

UN-HABITAT also confirms that:

> The wealth generated by cities does not automatically lead to poverty reduction; on the contrary intra-city-inequalities are on the rise, particularly in the cities of Africa and Latin America ... urbanization in many developing countries, particularly in sub-Saharan Africa, has not been accompanied by economic growth, industrialization or even development *per se*, the population of some African cities has grown despite poor economic growth.
>
> (UN-HABITAT, 2006, p. 48)

For example, Kinshasa in the Democratic Republic of Congo is now one of the largest cities in the world, with a population of over ten million people. Its economic base is almost entirely defined through the informal economy and the complex survival strategies of its inhabitants (de Boeck and Plissart, 2004). The economic inequalities embedded within contemporary global urbanisation are more than ones of income and wealth. They are underpinned by significant inequalities in access to basic forms of public infrastructure and, in particular, those associated with water and sanitation. As Beall (2002) points out:

The urban poor might only have access to water of poor quality or have to purchase it at high prices from private vendors. They often suffer the indignities of inadequate sanitation such as lack of privacy, or worse, ill health as a result of unhygienic conditions of the effects of urinary retention, especially on the part of women. Many poor people rely for bathing, laundering and defecation on draining channels, canals and rivers.

(Beall, 2002, p. 93)

Figure 5.4
Kinshasa and the urban poor

2.2 From social problems to economic opportunity and self-help

As Gerry Mooney argued in Chapter 4, slum-dwellers have traditionally been identified in academic and policy literatures as problem people. Even when not identified as morally responsible for their own poverty, their behaviour has often, nevertheless, been seen as dysfunctional. For example, Oscar Lewis has suggested that slum-dwelling, be it in developed or developing countries, is underpinned by a 'culture of poverty'. He suggests that the survival strategies developed by poor people themselves ultimately make it more difficult for them to escape from poverty. Describing the position of one poor family living in the slums of Mexico City, Lewis argues that it has adjusted effectively to its 'life condition': 'The parents show little drive to improve their standard of living and do not place high value on education, clothing, or cleanliness for themselves or their children' (Lewis, 1976, p. 15). In other words, they are trapped in a vicious cycle of poor living conditions, compounded by low expectations and particular behavioural patterns that reinforce their chronic economic insecurity.

These depictions of urban slum-dwellers as problem populations and slums as problem places sit uncomfortably with an emphasis on the importance of urban areas in economic and social development: 'Cities make countries rich. Countries that are highly urbanized tend to have higher incomes, more stable economies, stronger institutions and are better able to withstand the volatility of the world economy' (UN-HABITAT, 2006, p. 46). This understanding reflects an approach to social policy that sees positive welfare outcomes flowing from economic growth and development, and it has provided the driving force underpinning global social policy (the policy pronouncements and measures of international organisations). The World Bank has, at least since the early 1970s, emphasised the role that cities can play in enabling wider development. Its urban policy places emphasis on cities as drivers of economic growth and is aimed to ensure 'that countries extract the most benefit from urbanization' (World Bank Infrastructure Group Urban Development, 2000, p. 6). Such approaches can also be traced in initiatives pointing to the potential of the slums and their inhabitants. In the 1970s, Turner (1976) highlighted the ways in which those living in slums were able to manage informal housing and argued that what was needed was no more than minimal state involvement in providing necessary infrastructure (e.g. to deal with sewage). Others, such as de Soto (2002, p. 32), have gone further to claim that 'the entrepreneurial ingenuity of the poor has created wealth on a large scale'.

The important point here is not to debate whether these approaches are 'right' or 'wrong' (although see Davis, 2006, for a powerful critique), but rather to highlight the approach that underlies them: slum-dwellers are not understood as passive victims, but as active agents who are responsible for managing their own lives. In other words, what was previously described as dysfunctional and part of the problem is redefined as a fundamental part of the solution. Rhetorically, at least, the emphasis is placed on capacity building and responsibilisation as key elements of this policy discourse. You have already met the concepts of capacity building, capability and responsibility in Chapter 3 in the context of the emergence of an emphasis on 'well-being' rather than 'equality' in some welfare states. For the purposes of the present discussion, a common feature of the social justice agendas of global agencies such as the World Bank and of UN programmes (particularly UN-HABITAT and the UN Development Programme) is an emphasis on self-help and measures to 'responsibilise' slum-dwellers to improve their life conditions. This involves mobilising the (latent) capacities of poor communities and populations, with a powerful stress on the importance of the informal sector – that is, those activities which lie outside the officially regulated economy, whether because they draw on self-help and exchange through family and community networks, or because buyers and sellers of goods do their best to avoid state regulation and taxation. Instead of identifying the survival strategies of the poor (as Lewis did) as necessarily condemning them to a culture of poverty, these strategies are seen to provide evidence that poor people can be major sources of energy and vitality – potential drivers of development, rather than brakes on it.

In policy terms, these understandings found an expression in plans for developing 'slum upgrading' launched by the Cities Alliance in 1999 and endorsed at the UN Millennium Summit in 2000. These plans identified 'wellsprings of entrepreneurial energy' within the slums, while recognising that 'their brutal physical conditions limit residents' ability to realize welfare improvements from their own efforts alone' (Cities Alliance, 1999, p. 2). The strategy of 'slum upgrading' represents a significant break with one favouring the demolition of slums. According to UN-HABITAT (2003, p. 127), 'Upgrading has significant advantages; it is not only an affordable alternative to clearance and relocation, but it also minimizes the disturbance to the social and economic life of the community'. And as the 2006–07 *State of the World's Cities* report suggests, 'helping the poor to become more integrated into the fabric of urban society is the only long-lasting and sustainable solution to the growing urbanization of poverty' (UN-HABITAT, 2006, p. xii). At the start of the twenty-first century, the World Bank's President Wolfensohn (2001, p. 46) was also talking of the importance of 'Empowering the people of the slums'. The broad model is one that moves away from the provision of 'handouts' and services to the poor to one that seeks to develop the abilities of people living in slums to help themselves and draw them into the process of economic growth.

Activity 5.3

What are the social justice implications of this 'new' approach to managing slum-dwelling populations? To help think this through, you may wish to go back to Chapter 1 (Section 5), where Janet Newman and Nicola Yeates discussed different ideas of social justice. You may also like to return to Chapter 3 (Section 2), and review the discussion of the implications of a shift in emphasis from equality towards well-being.

Comment

Urban slums can be seen as prime sources of inequality because of the way in which they leave people in poverty and limit access to adequate housing and clean water. Building on the arguments of Chapter 1, we might expect policy responses to focus on the unequal distribution of resources and promote (as Rawls suggested) more equal access to forms of economic security through progressive distributive policies. In many ways, though, the 'new' approach taken by these international organisations is more consistent with the well-being approach outlined in Chapter 3, which emphasises the need to enable the poor to escape from poverty through their own initiative and remove the obstacles to their being able to do so. The vision of social justice is one which emphasises capacity building – providing people with the skills and abilities to improve their own lives, collectively or individually. Yet as Chapters 1 and 3 both indicated, self-help alone cannot solve problems of inequality where access to basic rights and resources are severely limited, so we may wish to doubt the effectiveness of a social justice strategy that does not include redistribution and state social guarantees. There is a further complication here in that, as far as the conditions of slums are concerned, the problem goes beyond the unequal distribution of income and wealth to also encompass unequal access to common resources such as air, water and land. This issue of common resources and how to manage them in the interests of everyone is one we explore further in the next section.

3 The problem of common resources

Thinking globally, we argued in the Introduction to this chapter, means thinking about ways in which we all inhabit a shared global space and are connected by globe-spanning networks, processes and resources. Inequalities in our access to, and use of, these resources often seem to be labelled a 'green issue' rather than a 'social issue'. But as the experience of New Orleans in the aftermath of Hurricane Katrina suggested (Chapter 4, Section 2), so-called global environmental problems and 'natural disasters' are manifestly *social* problems and disasters with causes and effects that reach far beyond locally affected areas and national borders. Here, then, we are confronted by a set of 'global' social challenges about how humanity as a whole manages its collective future through the management of common resources such as water, air and natural habitats.

In this context, the overlapping and interconnecting relationships between welfare and crime control emerge in unfamiliar but equally significant ways. Building on Chapters 1 and 3 which introduced the notion of social harm, in this section we explore the uncertain borders between social harm and crime control. To do so, the following case studies illustrate some of the ways in which people's lives and natural environments may be affected by the business priorities of multinational corporations. They also demonstrate how the things we purchase in our everyday lives (from denim clothing to flowers) come to our supermarkets and retail stores at a substantial cost to distant societies and environments.

3.1 The problem of the global 'commons': the case of the Amazon Rainforest

The first case study focuses on the Amazon Rainforest. The rainforest has become a symbol of global interconnectedness – it is widely agreed that its survival is necessary to counter global warming and climate change and to ensure the survival of humanity. In this context, however, what matters is how its management relates to issues of social justice and policy.

Figure 5.5
Commercial logging
and deforestation in
Brazil

Activity 5.4

The important questions are:

- Why does it matter that the rainforest is at risk?

- Who is affected by its destruction?

- What policy responses might be appropriate to manage it more effectively and more fairly?

Read the following extract with these questions in mind.

Extract 5.1

The Amazon Rainforest

The Amazon Rainforest is a 5.5 million hectare ecological wonderland located across seven South American nations. It is a natural resource that is continually subject to deforestation. The logging of the world's native forests – rainforests, jungles, etc. – is a crucial issue connected to global biodiversity and social justice. More than 50 per cent of the earth's species live in native forests and are constantly threatened by extinction because of habitat loss due to logging.

The rain forest supplies humans with food and medicines, and promotes the ongoing growth of flora and fauna. The loss of biodiversity would, then, have a significant impact far beyond the region. In addition, 50 per cent of all the oxygen we breathe comes from the rainforests; hence they are a major life source for all oxygen breathing animals. Deforestation is a major pollutant of the earth's atmosphere. The World Resources Institute (1997) estimates that native forests around the world store an estimated 433 billion tonnes of carbon – which is equivalent to the same amount of carbon dioxide produced by fossil fuel burning for the next 60 years. Loss of native forests has resulted in large-scale climatic change – for example, increased flooding in the sub-continent and South America. Native forests help maintain the environmental conditions that make life possible – including hydrolic cycles to global climate. The logging of the Amazon and natural rainforests is causing a hundred species to disappear each month around the world. Moreover, 40 per cent of our pharmaceuticals come from the rainforest. However, only 1 per cent of the plants have been assessed for their medical value. We are driving species into extinction before we have identified them. In addition, there are 7000 plants that human beings utilise for food – yet an estimated 75,000 are edible but not integrated within our food chain. Forests provide a substantial source of untapped food for human consumption.

Adapted by authors from The Nature Conservancy, 2007

Comment

This extract – which draws on widely available data – demonstrates how natural resources found in sites such as the Amazon Rainforest contribute to the health and welfare of populations across the globe. But these resources have particular consequences for those whose livelihoods and culture depend on them. Deforestation is often cited as an act of 'culturecide', defined as 'processes that have been purposely introduced that result in the decline or demise of a culture without necessarily resulting in the physical destruction of its bearers. [Culturecide] can involve some or all of the following: political and social institutions, culture, language, national feelings, religion, economic stability, personal security, liberty, health and dignity' (Stein, 2003). How is the destruction of the Amazon Rainforest influencing lives and culture? About 50 million indigenous peoples currently live in tropical rainforest. By 2020, at the current rate of logging, it is estimated that there will be no indigenous people living in their natural rainforest habitat. Not only does deforestation threaten the livelihoods and culture of indigenous peoples, but, as such peoples are argued to be the guardians of biodiversity, their extinction means the permanent loss of their knowledge and protection of the environment.

Given the importance of the Amazon and other natural rainforests, it is important to consider whether it is enough for such ecological treasures to be 'owned' by any given nation state (or acceptable that they should be systematically destroyed by mass timber-logging operations by corporations) – or whether such natural resources should be protected by collectively demarcating them as 'international parklands'. Such issues around access to and use of natural resources also open up significant questions about welfare beyond the confines of welfare states, and the ways in which 'environmental' struggles to protect the ecological systems that support livelihoods, medicines and life forms on which humans depend can be seen as key aspects of social justice struggles. Finally, they suggest ways in which the despoiling of the environment stretches our view of what constitutes a crime. We pursue these questions in Section 4.

3.2 Global markets and global corporations: jeans, flowers and environmental degradation in Kenya

The second case study focuses on the position of Kenya in the production process of two sets of consumer goods, which find their way into shops in Europe and North America. The case study is organised around a linked activity, and based upon two newspaper reports. The first report is concerned with the extraction of living organisms for use in the production of denim jeans, and the second with the growth and packaging of flowers for export.

Activity 5.5

In reading the two newspaper extracts, we would like you to consider:

■ What do they tell us about the ways in which the actions of powerful corporations may dramatically affect people's lives, even if that is not their intention?

■ How do apparently unconnected events and practices work together to shape the world in which we live, and how do they generate and maintain social inequality and injustice?

You should also think about the extracts as potential sources of evidence. There are two particular issues to consider here. The first relates to the way in which the newspapers themselves treat evidence – what is it about these extracts that makes them persuasive or convincing? Second, it would be worth thinking about whether there might be any difference between the sorts of evidence that would be expected for academic research and what would be acceptable in a journalistic piece. What does that mean for the way in which we, in turn, draw on newspapers for evidence?

In 2004, the *East African* magazine published a story that revealed that Western scientists had illegally taken samples of living organisms from Lake Bogoria in Kenya's Great Rift Valley (Mbaria, 2004). The scientists were reported to have sold the organisms to the biotechnology company, Genencor International, which in turn extracted an enzyme and sold it to Procter & Gamble for use as a bleaching agent in the production of denim clothing. The two companies have made millions of dollars from this indigenous Kenyan organism, and have retail outlets all around the world, yet the peoples of Kenya's Rift Valley region have not received any benefits.

Extract 5.2

Kenya loses Sh70m to biopirates

It now emerges that Rift Valley residents have, in the last two years, lost more than Sh70 million to western piracy targeting indigenous plants. This follows revelations that the detergent behind the faded jeans' fashion industry is derived from an indigenous plant that was pirated from the Rift Valley's caustic lakes.

International press now have bared how a British scientist from Leicester University worked with US firm Genencor to patent-utilise, without consent, a microbe that lives in the caustic lakes of Kenya's Rift Valley.

It was discovered that when jeans are washed with the 'stolen' microbe results in the production of an enzyme that fades the indigo dye thus giving them a natural faded look.

According to market monitoring research in the fashion industry, it is estimated that for the last one year, the company has made more than $1m (Sh73 million) in sales to detergent makers and textile firms. ...

This form of new thievery of Africa's resources falls under the category of biopiracy. The US-based Edmonds Institute recently published a report listing more than 30 examples of western medical, horticultural and cosmetic products it alleged had been 'pirated' from Africa.

An analysis of these patents by *The Observer* reveals that the Syngenta patent is one of seven granted by the UK authorities that now face accusations of biopiracy. These include: a diabetes drug being developed by a British firm that comes from the Libyan plant Artemisia judaica, an immunosuppressant drug being developed by GlaxoSmithKline that originates from a compound found in a termite hill in Gambia, a treatment for HIV/Aids taken from mycobacteria discovered in mud samples from the Lango district of central Uganda, infection-fighting drugs made from amoebas in Mauritius and

Venezuela, an anti-diarrhoea vaccine developed from Egyptian microbes and a slug barrier made from a Somalian species of myrrh.

...

... [T]he Brazilian ambassador to London, Jose Mauricio Bustani, described biopiracy as 'a silent disease'. He said: 'It is hardly detectable, it frequently does not leave traces and is an elusive activity perpetrated and often abetted by many well-known multinational companies. ...

Hoodia is a cactus-like African plant used by the San bushmen in South Africa to ward off hunger before hunting trips. Phytopharm has since linked with Unilever to market this product and currently is being developed as a diet drug. Unilever has agreed to pay up to £21m (Sh1.533 billion) to Phytopharm, which originally claimed the San tribe was extinct.

Through unrelenting activism from international human rights organisations and lawyers, the San community has managed to be incorporated into a fragile benefit-sharing agreement that will see it collect a small share of any profits realised. ...

...

James Shikwati, director, Inter-Region Economic Network (IREN-Kenya) writes, 'Lack of systematic recording and beyond a collective level of property right recognition, robbed many innovators in Africa the ability to have their ideas improved upon and made economically viable. More so, the lack of a property rights regime that could measure the countries that later colonised Africa made it easier for both physical and intellectual property to be seized by the occupying powers.'

Muiruri, 2006

Comment

This extract provides several examples of the ways in which global corporations exploit the indigenous flora and fauna of Africa for commercial gain. It highlights the extent to which apparently unrelated shifts in demand for particular goods (such as that for distressed or faded denim in Western fashion markets) can raise fundamental ethical questions about rights to naturally occurring phenomena in other countries. As the article reports, similar issues are raised in the development of a wide variety of drugs. This brings together powerfully a series of concerns linking social policy and issues of criminality. One of these relates to the way in which such activities may impact on the possibilities of poverty alleviation – making it possible for citizens of countries such as Kenya to benefit from a development strategy that draws on their natural resources. It looks as if current arrangements make it difficult to do that, although the experience of the San tribe suggests that some opportunities may exist. Another concern is explicitly raised by Jose Mauricio Bustani and James Shikwati, both of whom identify the actions of the corporations involved in terms of criminality (biopiracy or the colonial seizure of physical and intellectual property). In other words, the possibilities of achieving social justice are fundamentally affected by the entanglements between issues relating to social welfare, and the definition and management of criminal behaviour.

The evidence provided in the newspaper article is, in many ways, very persuasive. The author calls on three main sources to support the story. The first is other media sources (the international press – *The Observer*); the second is academic and other research publications (market-monitoring research – the Edmonds Institute); the third is interviews with, or quotations from, experts (the Brazilian ambassador to London; the director of IREN-Kenya). There is also reference to one particular case where the source is not directly identified but the information is relatively easily confirmable (relating to Hoodia, Phytopharm and the San tribe).

This looks, in other words, like a report in which we can place reasonable trust. But clearly the journalist is more concerned with producing an argument that grabs the reader's attention than with undertaking balanced investigation. In considering the helpfulness of any evidence of this sort, it is important to consider whose voice is being heard and (in this case, probably more important) also to consider from which position the evidence is being selected. Clearly the author is taking a critical stance towards the pharmaceutical corporations involved and has selected his sources accordingly. That does not mean that what has been written is 'wrong' or even misleading, but rather that it may be important to look for other sources against which the broad argument might be tested.

An academic piece of research on the same subject would have required rather clearer referencing so that readers could identify the sources of evidence (and confirm that they were robust). It would also have required some consideration of how the other agencies involved in the process saw their roles (e.g. it might be important to understand how Genencor or Phytopharm justified their behaviour). It would also have been interesting to explore the response of those international agencies which might have been expected to oversee the trade underlying the developments being considered. In other words, an academic paper might lead to the same conclusions and raise similar questions but it would need to be underpinned by more robust and extensive research.

This extract, drawing on experiences in Kenya, highlights the linkages between everyday decisions in countries like the UK and development elsewhere. We pursue this theme below in the next extract.

Figure 5.6
Fashion, flowers and the exploitation of Africa

Every 14 February many people throughout the UK celebrate Valentine's Day where the giving of flowers has become a common custom. Many of the fresh flowers that are bought in the UK are grown on the shores of Lake Naivasha in Kenya. In Extract 5.3, taken from an article published in *The Guardian*, Ochieng Ogodo and John Vidal report on some of the ecological and human costs of Valentine's Day.

As you read it, keep in mind the broad questions posed for this activity relating to social justice and inequality. You should also be thinking about the nature of the evidence provided in the extract and the reasons for its selection.

Extract 5.3

Drained of life

Thirty years ago, hippos and Maasai cattle herders shared the shoreline of Lake Naivasha in the Rift Valley of Kenya with the small local community of farmers and fishermen. The lake was judged one of the 10 top sites for birds in the world; its acacia and euphorbia trees were famed for their beauty; and its clear, fresh waters were abundant with fish. The human census in 1969 showed just 27,000 people living in the surrounding areas.

...

Giant greenhouses

The most visible changes to the lake in the past 30 years, and the cause of much of its problems, are the giant sheds and greenhouses of more than 50 major flower farms that now line its shores, and the settlements of more than 250,000 people who have flooded into the area since the global flower industry moved in. Naivasha is now Europe's prime source of cut flowers and, to a lesser extent, vegetables, which are grown on more than 50 sq km of land around the lake in the open and under 2,000 hectares (4,943 acres) of plastic.

...

... Picked in the morning, the flowers can be packed, refrigerated and on their way by plane to Britain by the afternoon. The UK imported 18,000 tonnes of flowers from Kenya in 2005, nearly twice the number in 2001. If you buy Valentine's Day roses today in Europe, there is a one in three chance that they will have been flown 6,000km from Kenya, and a pretty good chance that they will be from Naivasha.

There are no publicly available figures on how much water the companies extract from the lake, but they are conservatively estimated to take, on average, at least 20,000 cubic metres of water a day. A survey by a Kenyan school last October found that the maximum depth of the lake was now just 3.7 metres, and that the level was more than three metres below what it was in 1982. ...

...

The real price of the flowers sent to Britain is incalculable, says one Kenyan conservationist, who asked not to be named following the murder last year of a woman who had fought to save the lake. 'What is not taken into account by the companies is that their activities place enormous extra pressure on the lake,' he says. 'It's not just the water that they extract. Nearly 40,000 people work in the farms around Lake

Naivasha, but every job attracts nearly seven other people to the area. We estimate that the new population uses about 750,000 bags of charcoal a year. The forests are being felled to provide fuel for the people growing the flowers.'

...

The flower farming has also encouraged overfishing, even as stocks are falling. John Onyango, a fisherman, says many of the companies dump raw effluent and chemicals into the lake. 'Lots of fish are dying as a result,' he says. 'I cannot get enough fish, compared to three years ago.'

...

Naivasha has hardly benefited from the farms, says the mayor, Musa Gitau. 'The population influx has stressed us in terms of garbage collection, sanitation, schools, electricity, hospitals and roads,' he says.

...

Child assaults

Gitau says the human influx has also affected education and crime rates. 'One school now has 2,800 pupils,' he says. 'And Naivasha has more rape cases and sexual assaults than any other town in the country. Barely a day passes without one or two cases of child assaults or rapes. This is because most mothers work at the farms and leave their children under the care of old women for a small fee.'

He says the farms owe the council more than 70m Kenyan shillings (£512,160) – funds that would go a long way to improving town services. 'Efforts to make them pay have been fruitless,' he says. '... The flower industry is a lucrative business with big money. The same money is given to politicians and top government officials as kickbacks, making the farmers untouchable.'

...

'We live like paupers'

The price of 12 red roses outside Cannon Street in London last week was nearly £10, and will be even more today. That's more than Achieng, a young woman who packs and cuts roses in one of the big flower farms around Lake Naivasha, earns in a week.

...

Akinyi, 29, who also works in the farms, says: 'Although some companies house their workers, when they do, they force families to live together. We are forced to live in one room and share it with another family, a situation that causes tensions and conflicts ... .'

...

The farms have widely varying health standards. The best have a hospital and full-time doctors, 'but the majority provide nothing', says Akinyi. 'One of my colleagues recently miscarried because of long exposure to the chemicals that are used on the flowers. The management should give us milk to minimise the effects, but they never do so. So we are always scratching ourselves because of the effects of the chemicals.'

...

Most workers earn about £23 a month and those who are not housed by the companies get a 'house allowance' of about £8. 'This wage is barely enough to meet basic needs such as school fees, travel, food, and medical costs,' Mwende, 27, says. 'You need at least £50 a month to live. So we work in the farms, but also look for alternatives such as selling peanuts and fish. I really struggle. We live like paupers.'

Ogodo and Vidal, 2007

Comment

The above extract provides evidence of various deep-rooted and everyday injustices. It also reminds us that certain cultural acts in our society have biographies and histories that may include the destruction of other societies and habitats. And they provide examples of what is now referred to as eco crime. An eco crime (often used synonymously with 'green crime' or 'environmental crime') is an act of 'environmental harm and ecological degradation' (Walters, 2005, p. 146). For Laura Westra (2004, p. 309), eco crime is unprovoked aggression, 'committed in the pursuit of other goals and "necessities" such as economic advantage'. Westra's work extends the definition of eco crime beyond ecological degradation to include human health, global security and justice. She suggests that eco crimes committed by governments and corporations in pursuit of free trade or progress are 'attacks on the human person' that deprive civilians (notably the poor) of the social, cultural and economic benefits of their environment. The European Court of Human Rights has ruled that all member states and their subjects have a 'right to a safe environment' (Mularoni, 2003). In other words, the issues at stake relate not just to the distribution of resources, but also to issues of recognition raised by Young (1990) as discussed in Chapter 1, Section 5.

In this extract, too, the evidence presented is very persuasive, but it relies on trust in the journalists who have undertaken the work and on the newspaper in which it is published. The extract starts with an engaging description referring to an almost idyllic past (hippos, Maasai cattle herders and a small local community of farmers and fishermen).

There is little direct reference to published sources (something one would expect in any piece of academic research), although there are several statements that seem to be based on official statistics or academic sources (relating to the population, the shrinkage of the lake, data on the scale of flower production and the scale of the trade, levels of water consumption, cost of flowers in London, levels of income of workers). The piece does draw on the expertise of one particular (unnamed) conservationist – in a journalistic context the inability to identify the expert by name almost strengthens the power of the argument (because it is risky to testify), and this highlights the risks that are sometimes associated with research that challenges powerful orthodoxies.

However, it would also be important in any piece of academic research to reinforce the evidence of this conservationist with evidence from other sources (and possibly primary research). As a piece of journalism, the strength of the argument is reinforced by a series of individual testimonies from ordinary people in Kenya (John Onyango, Achieng, Akinyi and Mwende). These are powerful sources and often it is only through in-depth interviews drawing on personal experience that it is possible to gain a good understanding of how societies are affected by processes like those under consideration in the article. But, of course, from a research point of view, the statements here are tantalisingly brief and we have no way of knowing how these particular individuals were chosen to be interviewed. In other words, this piece does provide strong evidence, but it also encourages us to ask further questions and look for ways of developing a stronger evidence base.

3.3 Identifying criminal behaviour

The three extracts in Section 3 have opened up important questions about the ways in which welfare and crime control policies are entangled in global social and economic relationships. At stake in such questions is how we define 'crime'. This is the focus of Activity 5.6.

Activity 5.6

One of the issues that runs through the case studies, but is not fully drawn out, relates to the extent to which the activities under discussion can be identified as criminal. Now read through the Kenyan case study extracts again with the following two questions in mind:

■ Which activities are defined as criminal but tend not to be prosecuted?

■ Which activities are not defined as criminal, but ought to be?

Comment

You may have found this activity difficult for at least two reasons. First, the idea of criminal behaviour tends to be thought of in terms of individual acts, rather than the acts of companies and commercial enterprises. But think back to the discussion in Chapter 3, Section 4 about how far the negligence of employers in relation to the safety and well-being of the workforce can be viewed in terms of 'harm' and 'crime'. Note also the discussion there about how far such negligence, even when defined as a crime, is successfully regulated through the criminal justice system. This takes us to the second difficulty: the danger that the crimes of the 'powerful' will be ignored, with emphasis instead being placed on the behaviour of poorer and less powerful people and on the management of 'dangerous' populations of one sort or another. In these cases, it is major corporations and their shareholders that seem to have benefited from activity that might be identified as criminal. In Extract 5.2, the argument seems to be that it should quite directly be identified as biopiracy and subject to international or national laws (although currently there are no laws in the area); while in Extract 5.3 it might be argued that the destruction of local environments should be identified as criminal, even if there is no direct and obvious criminal intent (buying roses for Valentine's Day).

When we refer to crimes of the powerful we are describing the illegal or harmful actions of states and corporations. In many instances the activities of corporations may commence as legal business practices, yet evolve into harmful and law-breaking conduct. Likewise, it is common for transnational corporate activity (that which operates across national borders) to violate laws in one country while operating legally in another. As a result, many scholars adopt a socio-legal analysis of corporate activity that includes an assessment of both law-breaking and 'harmful' activity.

Michalowski (1985, p. 314) defines corporate crime as '[a]ctions that are either prohibited by law or that knowingly lead to social injury, taken by official representatives of legitimate businesses to facilitate capital accumulation within those businesses'.

As a result, examining the actions of powerful individuals, groups and entities requires an approach that does not take their claims at face value but subjects them to scrutiny (Pearce, 2003, p. xi). When reading the case studies we should be mindful that 'crimes committed by states and corporations have far greater economic, physical and social costs than those associated with "conventional" criminals who continue to represent the fixation of contemporary criminal justice systems' (Tombs and Whyte, 2003, p. 3). Infinitely more human tragedy and suffering, and more environmental destruction, is caused by the behaviours of those in positions of 'trust' than by those people who are prosecuted and sentenced to prison.

4   Reframing justice?

This chapter has highlighted a number of ways in which the notion of global social justice points up the limitations of a national framing of justice and its institutionalisation in the form of welfare states. Justice – both social and criminal – tends to apply to 'domestic' populations. The fundamental question remains whether and how it might be applied to everyone, irrespective of the country in which they happen to be born or to live. This has been the focus of a great deal of debate, in which a range of distinctive positions have been adopted (see Yeates, 2008 for further discussion).

Here we want to explore another way into these questions, which explicitly draws on notions of 'justice'. In everyday language, justice is often associated with the rule of law and the operation of the courts, and it might be helpful to think through some of the issues with which we have been concerned. International justice has been developed as a set of rules governing relations between states, but notions of transnational justice are now beginning to be taken more seriously within debates about how to manage our common affairs collectively. A range of transnational legal processes are emerging through protocols and interstate agreements that seek to regulate and prevent illicit corporate activity within the complex webs of global markets (Likosky, 2002).

Environmental justice is one important area in which we can see these transnational legal processes at work. As you saw earlier in this chapter, environmental justice is widely accepted as imperative for future ecological and human security (see also **Cochrane and Talbot, 2008**). Chambers and Green (2005) argue that the growing number of international environmental agreements and institutions (exceeding 500) has occurred simultaneously with a proliferation of environmental degradation. What is needed, they argue, is a new and integrated system of environmental governance that mobilises and coordinates existing international resources around questions of environmental sustainability. An international environmental court has been mooted to facilitate such a system. In 2002, at the World Summit on Sustainable Development, 130 senior judges from around the world identified that there were sufficient domestic and international laws to protect the environment, but that a growing number of 'miscreant corporations and backsliding governments' were unwilling to self-regulate or enforce laws. The judges called for a unified international court of the environment to strengthen the existing legal framework of environmental protection, a measure which would also protect the world's poor who are 'often the hardest-hit victims of environmental crimes' (quoted in James, 2002, p. 1).

Further insistence on the need for an international environment court was recommended at the Conference of the Americas for the Environment and Sustainable Development at Rio de Janeiro in September 2004. In a country continually exploited for its genetic diversity and richness, the Brazilian Government continues to support an international legal forum that can prosecute and sanction criminal activities that have origins and backing beyond Brazil's jurisdiction. The UN, through its environment programme and, notably, the World Environmental Organization see the role of a new system of environmental governance as necessitating a mixture of precaution, education, responsibility and control. Such a system is about providing legal leadership for nation states to develop their own regulatory frameworks for dealing with environmental (in)security and social (in)justice. In some respects, just as in the case of hate crime discussed by **Fergusson and Muncie (2008)**, the role of the law and of the court would be symbolic, as much as practical; that is, changes in behaviour in the context of a new legal framework might be more significant than the imposition of any penalties through the court process. Moreover, such measures are about harm minimisation that can be achieved through dispute resolution and notions of restorative justice (Postiglione, 2004).

Activity 5.7

What do you think might be the advantages and disadvantages of setting up a World Environmental Court? In responding to this question, you might also like to look back to Chapter 3 and the discussion in Section 4 of the advantages and disadvantages of state laws protecting workers from harm in the workplace. In the light of this, you could think about:

- How much power do you think such global institutions might actually carry, when faced with nation states which protect their own authority and rights to manage events occurring within their borders?

- How might the decisions of such a court be implemented and policed?

- What other strategies could be developed to help reduce environmental harm and crime?

Comment

It might be argued that a World Environmental Court could work as a more general model for achieving global social justice. Similar comments could be made with regard to the international funding and policy bodies discussed in Section 2 of this chapter. However, institutional approaches along these lines also have significant weaknesses. In practice they remain tied into international networks, dependent on the whims of powerful nations. It is also difficult to see what the policing mechanisms to enforce the decisions might be. The difficulties associated with various UN military missions provide one example of this. There is also a danger that this would be social justice from the top down and that it is likely that it would be difficult to sustain, since the most powerful agencies with a global presence are unlikely to be those most committed to social justice, particularly if its pursuit undermines their position and interests.

Figure 5.7
Demonstrating against corporate pollution

There will, it seems, continue to be challenges to the achievement of global social justice when the most powerful nations (economically and militarily) abuse the rights of others and ignore international law. So, it may instead be more helpful to consider the ways in which global social justice might be achieved through various interconnected pathways both within and outside formal state or judicially based avenues of regulation. From this perspective, justice may need to be pursued and achieved outside of legal domains (justice beyond the courtroom), as well as within it. For example, the mobilisation of resistance against poverty is central to international policies that seek to eradicate poverty. Likewise, other forms of citizen participation or protest in areas involving the environment, trade and migration are ways through which injustices are identified, and subsequently addressed. As a result, it may be helpful to consider mobilisations for global social justice as diffuse, multi-actor networks rather than as a single institution. These mobilisations are not just about the coordinated actions of various states, international bodies and non-governmental organisations: they also concern the development of networks where individuals themselves form alliances and pockets of localised resistance to voice concerns about inequality and exploitation and act to remedy them.

5   Review: globalising social justice

This chapter is not intended to provide a blueprint for achieving global social justice. Rather, it has been our purpose to begin to explore the differences it makes to think about adding the prefix 'global' to the discussion of social justice. We have sought to understand the world as a single global social system in which events in one place are quickly relayed to and impact upon others. Instead of simply seeing the world as a series of national 'societies', we have started from an understanding of the world as one society, constituted by the networks and relationships that cut across territorial boundaries. It is the coming together of a range of actors in such networks that gives us a new perspective of the global context of social injustice. So, for example, the deforestation of the Amazon Rainforest discussed earlier is not simply the result of some wilful action of the Brazilian Government to permit timber corporations to log ancient indigenous woodlands. Deforestation in the Amazon is a global process that involves producers and consumers from around the world. The harmful felling of Amazon trees occurs because of a network of participating agents – from the lumberjack who controls the saw to the British family that spreads the chipwood across their front garden. All combine and contribute to the act of deforestation. This shift in emphasis is important for the study of social justice and for exploring the ways in which policies relating to social welfare and crime control come together and interact.

Thinking globally draws our attention not only to the reach or extent of social, economic and environmental problems, but also to the interdependence of places and phenomena that we often experience as disconnected. It requires us to look beyond national boundaries to the arena of global agencies and intergovernmental organisations (such as the World Bank, the United Nations, the G8 and the European Union) and international non-governmental organisations such as Oxfam and Greenpeace. Moreover, we cannot understand the factors that both obstruct and facilitate global social justice unless we consider the role of multinational corporations. Here, we have argued, notions of crime and crime control might be refocused on the powerful rather than the poor. It is, after all, the crimes of the rich and powerful that have the most far-reaching, adverse impacts upon our quality of life. This is not to discount the actions of 'ordinary people' in mobilising against injustice wherever it is manifested, or the importance of networks that connect different kinds of protest movements – both of which are crucial ways of developing norms of social justice that transcend national borders.

All of this has taken us back to some of the concepts you met in earlier chapters of this book. Although the possibility of redistribution (following the principles enunciated by Rawls) (Chapter 1, Section 5) has had some part to play in these debates, it is apparent that global social structures and institutional context substantially limit what is possible, as Young (1990) notes. Our discussion of possible judicial routes forward illustrates how contexts and structures might be changed (as well as the difficulties in doing so). We have also highlighted the importance of recognition (identified by Young) and its role in underpinning 'new' judicial processes associated with transnational justice. This chapter has also discussed the global aspects of concepts such as harm, equality and well-being that were introduced in Chapters 2 and 3. In Section 2 we examined how international organisations such as the UN and the World Bank seem to have taken up ideas around well-being that have become more prominent in recent years. While these may signal a more positive evaluation and recognition of the attributes and abilities of populations living in slums, such ideas tend to place the onus on slum-dwellers to help themselves out of poverty and integrate into 'normal' society and 'mainstream' economic activity, while providing only minimal state support. We also considered in that context the possible limitations of measures to redistribute income and wealth in a context where inequalities extend to unequal access to common resources.

A global perspective on social justice brings together a combination of issues, including ethics and debt, world poverty and global health, environmental and sustainable development, human rights and fair trade policies. In that sense, it also returns us to some of the key questions raised in Chapter 1; in particular, to the implications of thinking about the social in social justice. The social, here, is not delimited by the boundaries of a particular society conceived of as a nation state. In a global context it opens up the need to conceive of relationships that stretch across the world, ideas that travel to different countries, common resources that are shared by humanity as whole, and new and better ways of managing our common affairs in the wider public interest.

Further reading

For further reading about the ways in which social policy has become globalised, we recommend the following sources. Nicola Yeates's (ed.) *Understanding Global Social Policy* (2008, The Policy Press) is an accessible student-oriented volume that examines the emergence and development of global social policy across a wide range of policy areas, including the ways in which population control thinking impacts on social welfare and crime control. Bob Deacon's *Global Social Policy and Governance* (2007, Sage) discusses the social welfare policies of international organisations, emphasising the implications of changing forms of social policy and governance for those seeking to build a fairer world. Both of these books contain helpful advice on further reading and resources for those wishing to explore debates more fully. Michael Cahill's *The Environment and Social Policy* (2002, Routledge) discusses the relationship between environmental issues and social policy, while Reece Walters's *Eco Crime and Genetically Modified Food* (2008, Routledge) brings scientific debates about genetics and agriculture into the social and criminological arenas. It critiques the harmful and illegal actions of corporations and governments in relation to the sale and production of GM food, highlights the limitations of existing policies of regulation and enforcement, and proposes pathways for justice within and beyond the courtroom.

References

Beall, J. (2002) 'Water supply and sanitation for sustainable cities' in Beall, J., Crow, B., Simon, S. and Wilson, G. (eds) *Sustainability*, Maidenhead, Open University Press/Milton Keynes, The Open University.

Castells, M. (1998) *End of Millennium*, Oxford, Blackwell.

Chambers, W. and Green, J. (eds) (2005) *Reforming International Environmental Governance: From Institutional Limits to Innovative Reforms*, Washington, DC, United Nations University Press.

Cities Alliance (1999) *Cities without Slums: Action Plan for Moving Slum Upgrading to Scale*, Washington DC, The World Bank/UNCS (HABITAT).

Cochrane, A. and Talbot, D. (2008) 'War, disease and human security' in Cochrane, A. and Talbot, D. (eds) *Security: Welfare, Crime and Society*, Maidenhead, Open University Press/Milton Keynes, The Open University.

Davis, M. (2006) *Planet of Slums*, London, Verso.

de Boeck, F. and Plissart, M-F. (2004) *Kinshasa: Tales of the Invisible City*, Gent, Ludion.

de Soto, H. (2002) *The Mystery of Capital: Why Capitalism Triumphs in the West and Fails Everywhere Else*, London, Black Swan.

Fergusson, R. and Muncie, J. (2008) 'Criminalising conduct?' in Cochrane, A. and Talbot, D. (eds) (2008) *Security: Welfare, Crime and Society*, Maidenhead, Open University Press/Milton Keynes, The Open University.

James, B. (2002) 'International judges: environmental laws not enforced', *International Herald Tribune*, 28 August, p. 1.

Lewis, O. (1976) *Five Families: Mexican Case Studies in the Culture of Poverty*, London, Souvenir Press.

Likosky, M. (ed.) (2002) *Transnational Legal Processes: Globalisation and Power Disparities*, London, Butterworth.

Mbaria, J. (2004) 'KWS seeks millions from Procter & Gamble', *East African*, Nairobi, 23 August.

Michalowski, R. (1985) *Order, Law and Power*, New York, NY, Random House.

Muiruri, M. (2006) 'Kenya loses Sh70m to biopirates', *Kenya Times*, 29 August.

Mularoni, A. (2003) 'The right to a safe environment in the case-law of the European Court of Human Rights' in Postiglione, A. (ed.) *The Role of the Judiciary in the Implementation and Enforcement of Environmental Law*, Rome, International Court of the Environmental Foundation.

The Nature Conservancy (2007) 'Rainforests: facts about rainforests' [online], http://www.nature.org/rainforests/explore/facts.html (Accessed 16 January 2008).

Ogodo, O. and Vidal, J. (2007) 'Drained of life', *The Guardian*, 14 February 2007 [online], http://www.guardian.co.uk/society/2007/feb/14/kenya.conservation (Accessed 3 December 2007).

Pearce, F. (2003) 'Holy wars and spiritual revitalization' in Tombs, S. and Whyte, D. (eds) (2003) *Unmasking Crimes of the Powerful: Scrutinizing States and Corporations*. New York, NY, Peter Lang.

Postiglione, A. (2004) *Need For An International Court Of The Environment*, Rome, International Court of the Environmental Foundation.

Stein, S. (2003) 'Culturecide' in Cashmore, E. (ed.) *Encyclopedia of Race and Ethnic Studies*, London, Routledge; Stein's definition of culturecide is also available online at http://www.ess.uwe.ac.uk/genocide/culturecide.htm (Accessed 10 December 2007).

Tombs, S. and Whyte, D. (eds) (2003) *Unmasking Crimes of the Powerful: Scrutinizing States and Corporations*, New York, NY, Peter Lang.

Turner, J. (1976) *Housing by People: Towards Autonomy in Building Environments*, London, Marion Boyars.

United Nations Human Settlements Programme (UN-HABITAT) (2003) *The Challenge of the Slums: Global Report on Human Settlements*, London, Earthscan.

United Nations Human Settlements Programme (UN-HABITAT) (2006) *The State of the World's Cities Report 2006/7. The Millennium Development Goals and Urban Sustainability: 30 Years of Shaping the Habitat Agenda*, London, Earthscan.

Walters, R. (2005) 'Eco crime' in McLaughlin, E. and Muncie, J. (eds) *The Sage Dictionary of Criminology*, London, Sage.

Westra, L. (2004) *Ecoviolence and the Law: Supranational Normative Foundations of Ecocrime*, Ardsley, NY, Transnational Publishers.

Wolfensohn, J. (2001) 'The World Bank and global city-regions: reaching the poor' in Scott, A. (ed.) *Global City-Regions: Trends, Theory, Policy*, Oxford, Oxford University Press.

World Bank Infrastructure Group Urban Development (2000) *Cities in Transition: World Bank Urban and Local Government Strategy*, Washington, DC, The World Bank.

World Resources Institute (1997) *The Last Frontier Forests: Ecosystems and Economies on the Edge*, Washington, DC, World Resources Institute.

Yeates, N. (ed.) (2008) *Understanding Global Social Policy*, Bristol, The Policy Press.

Young, I.M. (1990) *Justice and the Politics of Difference*, Princeton, NJ, Princeton University Press.

Chapter 6
Conclusion

Janet Newman and Nicola Yeates

Contents

1   Introduction

This book has focused on social justice because of its enduring and widespread appeal among social scientists, policymakers, popular movements and ordinary citizens around the world. The idea of social justice has shaped how many people understand the nature of society and the patterns of injustice or disadvantage that they see and experience. It has also informed social and political struggles to bring about a better society – one in which resources, rewards and burdens are distributed more equitably, and people are treated with more care, respect and dignity. In this book social justice has been found to be a particularly useful concept in illuminating responses to social problems such as inequality, poverty, social exclusion and harm. And it has also helped us to explore the connections between welfare, crime and society in a range of contexts around the world, past and present.

We begin this concluding chapter by returning to the four aims of the book set out in Chapter 1. These were to:

- introduce 'social justice' as a normative concept and a mobilising idea – one that has helped shape struggles against inequality and injustice

- examine the social basis of social justice, including the ways in which ideas about justice and injustice are both changeable and contested

- look at how a focus on social justice can reveal some of the ways in which social welfare and crime control policies are entangled

- provide an appreciation of the importance of evidence and help you to assess different kinds of evidence.

This final chapter looks across the book as a whole in the light of these aims. This chapter:

- reviews how these aims have been addressed

- reviews specific chapters

- reflects on the concepts, evidence forms and arguments that have run through the book.

We focus in particular on the problem of defining what we mean when we talk about the social in social justice (Section 2); return to the theme of 'entanglement' that has been discussed in different chapters (Section 3); and review some of the kinds of evidence used in developing the analysis of notions of social justice (Section 4). Section 5 returns to the idea of contestation and change, and Section 6 offers some observations on what we might term the politics of social justice.

Across the chapters the authors have highlighted different struggles, in different periods, and in different places – from the movements against apartheid in South Africa in the twentieth century to protests against environmental degradation in the twenty-first. In doing so they have shown how social justice is not a static concept; it is a dynamic, changing one. As such, they have not tried to tie it down with a single definition, but have stressed how multidimensional it is.

Activity 6.1

Each chapter has explored different dimensions of social justice and injustice, and shown how it has been mobilised in different contexts for different purposes.

Look back through the chapters at the core concepts and think about what dimensions of social (in)justice they help illuminate, and what kinds of mobilisations against injustice have arisen in response. Table 6.1 makes a start at this, and you are invited to develop the table by adding to your own larger copy of it as you review each chapter.

Table 6.1 Dimensions of social (in)justice

Chapter	Dimensions of social justice/injustice	Social justice as a mobilising idea
Chapter 1: Making social justice: ideas, struggles and responses	Inequality Discrimination	Responses to personal experiences of injustice
Chapter 2: Looking for social justice: welfare states and beyond	Inequality Social exclusion	Social movement struggles, and the making of welfare states
Chapter 3: Well-being, harm and work	Harm Well-being	Mobilisations against the harms perpetrated by the powerful over the powerless
Chapter 4: 'Problem' populations, 'problem' places	Poverty Disadvantage	Protest and dissent on the part of those defined as 'problem populations' living in 'problem places'
Chapter 5: The globalisation of social justice	Environmental harm Unequal access to common resources	Development of transnational protest networks; calls for global governance reform

Comment

Column 2 in this table shows how social justice is multidimensional. That is, it is not 'just' about overcoming one kind of injustice. But identifying dimensions of social injustice in this way is not only about continually adding new categories of injustice on to a list of issues requiring policy attention. Rather, we want to highlight the relationships between different dimensions of injustice. For example, the experience of poverty may well be intensified by acts of discrimination on the part of schools, employers, governments and other institutions. Those experiencing disadvantage and social exclusion as 'problem' people in 'problem' places may well be more susceptible to a range of harms, including environmental harms.

Column 3 depicts some of the mobilisations against different dimensions of social justice that have been discussed in earlier chapters. But the relationship between columns 2 and 3 is not simple and direct: mobilisations depend on the processes debated in Chapter 2 that make inequality and injustice *visible, contestable* and *changeable*.

Different chapters have noted a number of examples of historical or current struggles for social justice (e.g. the civil rights struggles discussed in Chapter 1, the protest movements in Chapter 2, the struggles of workers against unjust or unhealthy working conditions in Chapter 3, the disturbances in the *banlieues* of France in Chapter 4, protests against 'eco' crimes in Chapter 5). This is why, in Chapter 1, we argued that ideas of social justice are both contested and changeable. What is viewed as the natural order of things today may be viewed as unenlightened, discriminatory or unjust tomorrow. This takes us to the importance of understanding the *social* basis of social justice.

2   What's social about social justice?

In Chapter 1 we argued that, while the experience of injustice is felt at a very personal level, we also need to understand the social dimensions of social justice. Throughout the book you have seen a range of struggles around what the social might mean and who can be a part of it. The civil rights struggles noted in Chapter 1 were struggles on the part of particular groups to be acknowledged as legitimate members of a society, with political and social, as well as legal, rights. The formation of welfare states discussed in Chapter 2 highlighted social struggles that produced new claims for resources – based on both recognition and redistribution – within particular societies. The globalisation of social justice traced in Chapter 5 expands the notion of what the social means, inviting us to think of ourselves as connected to others around the world and to be concerned about global patterns of membership, ownership and resource distribution.

By adding the word 'social' to 'justice', then, the chapter authors are distinguishing it from a narrower conception of justice associated with treatment under the law. As you have seen, legal measures – and the institutions that enforce them – are significant in protecting rights and freedoms. But justice under the law has its roots in wider conceptions of social justice. For example, the laws on equality discussed in Chapter 2, or on workplace safety debated in Chapter 3, did not arise from nowhere – they were each based on social struggles that gave rise to forms of social change and legal innovations. Changes in the law may, at times, help bring about social change by affirming symbolically the importance of particular ideas, but legal measures need to be supported by other social processes to make them effective. This issue was debated explicitly in Chapter 3, where the limits of formal workplace regulation were discussed, and in Chapter 5, where the authors invited you to consider the strengths and limitations of the idea of a global environmental court.

In focusing on *social* justice the chapter authors are also making a claim that social justice is not just about individuals. Individualised conceptions of justice are related to legal justice, but have a broader reach in notions of 'fair treatment', 'entitlements' and 'rights'. Again, each of these is important – but redressing unfairness for a specific individual will do little to challenge the broader patterns of disadvantage, exclusion or harm that produced their experience of injustice in the first place. This is why the focus has often been on social groups – recognised collectivities based on class, gender, 'race', and so on – and the systematic patterns of unfairness or inequality that they may experience.

The social basis of social justice also lies in commonly held ideas and values (e.g. the 'moral economy' discussed in Chapter 1, Section 6). Here we can understand social justice as a normative concept: a concept that suggests what *ought* to happen, how people *should* behave towards and treat one another. Such norms are socially communicated and so help shape personal beliefs and actions. This in turn raised questions about the institutions and policies that embody and protect the norms and ethical commitments of a particular society. For example, Chapter 2 traced the ways in which the formation of welfare states rested on particular compromises and settlements between different social groups.

This opens up once again the question of who gets to be part of the social entity in which norms of justice are developed and institutionally embedded. Throughout the book, but particularly in Chapter 4, the authors have traced patterns of marginalisation and exclusion which place particular groups of people 'outside' the reach of norms and institutions of social justice, even when they live within the same state or nation. But they have also challenged the idea of the nation state as the territorial boundary that delimits the reach of norms and institutions of social justice. In Chapter 5 you met the concept of 'the commons' as a way of depicting a much broader, global, sense of the social – one that highlights the significance of access to and ownership of basic resources such as air, water and land, and that stresses our common responsibility for the globe we inhabit.

Social justice is, then, a device for challenging particular forms of inequality or unfairness, and a way of summoning up moral, ethical and political commitments to norms and values about how a society – however defined – should be organised. But where the ideas and norms of one group clash with those of another, what is viewed as just and unjust is no longer a simple matter; and such clashes may lead to contestation, dissent or protest, as you have seen. This leads to a highlighting of the dynamic qualities of social justice, and its implications for our understanding of social change. You have seen that social justice can be a mobilising idea, producing dissent and opening up new claims for resources and recognition. But patterns of social change – in particular new strategies for 'managing and governing populations' – may also close down the spaces in which claims for social justice are mobilised and voiced. This points to the next topic – the entanglement of welfare and crime control.

3   Untangling 'entanglement': social justice, social welfare and crime control

In this book, its authors have used the idea of 'entanglement' to suggest that relationships between different policies, practices and processes of change are not clear-cut. They work with – and against – each other, sometimes in mutually reinforcing ways, at other moments interacting negatively. This is most vividly illustrated in the relationship between welfare and crime control strategies.

In Chapter 1 we argued that issues of inequality, poverty and social exclusion cut across both social welfare and crime control domains, and noted that while some responses to these issues may become the focus of social welfare policies, others may become the focus of crime control interventions. Social justice, then, is neither the exclusive terrain of social welfare nor of crime control. Indeed, the boundaries between these two domains tend to be mobile and porous.

We introduced this idea of entanglement in Chapter 1, arguing that the neat distinction between the goals of social welfare (social well-being) and the goals of crime control (maintaining social order) break down on closer inspection. Each of the chapters has taken up this issue of the extensive entanglement of social welfare and crime control strategies and provision.

Activity 6.2

At this point, we invite you to look back over the chapters and remind yourself of how each author has described and discussed the entanglements between welfare and crime control. Table 6.2 sets out some examples as a starting point. But these entanglements do not all take the same form. As you add to the table and remind yourself of the examples, please think about the *different* ways in which entanglement is discussed.

Table 6.2 The entangled relationships between social welfare and crime control

Chapter 1: Section 4	Crime control measures impact adversely on social welfare and produce justice struggles. State withdrawal from the direct provision of welfare services is accompanied by greater attention to 'antisocial' behaviour of younger and poorer groups in society
Chapter 1: Sections 3 and 6	Dissent and protest against social injustice may be the subject of criminalising responses
Chapter 2: Section 2	Welfare states are involved in the maintenance of social order and stability by naturalising and normalising social inequalities
Chapter 2: Sections 2, 3, 4	Welfare states prescribe certain ideas of behaviour ('norms' of good conduct). These may stigmatise certain categories of people – in Booth's study, the poor; and, in the twenty-first century, those who are not gainfully employed or who do not comply with norms of active citizenship. Welfare states also 'police' adherence to norms of good conduct and may punish those who deviate from them. Punishments may range from measures such as the withdrawal of benefits and services to actual criminalisation
Chapter 3: Section 3	'Care' – whether provided informally (in the home) or through welfare states – can involve the abuse, neglect and exploitation of vulnerable people. Some abuses are subject to criminal prosecution

Table 6.2 (continued)

Chapter 3: Section 4	Treaties, conventions, laws and workers' rights are often ineffective in regulating safety and ensuring freedom from harm in the workplace. Trade unions have attempted to limit workplace harms by pursuing rights and legal safeguards, but their power has been weakened. In an attempt to avoid legislative action, some companies are now developing voluntary codes of conduct based on the idea of social responsibility
Chapter 4: Section 2	'Problem populations' in 'problem places' – such as the black population of New Orleans – tend to be stigmatised, viewed as a source of harm, crime and social disorder
Chapter 4: Section 3	Some of the case studies show how welfare policies that sought to solve housing problems in the past have had damaging consequences, leading to punitive and criminalising policies in the present
Chapter 5: Section 2	'Global slums' are sites of concerns about crime and disorder. They are also sites of emerging understandings about how slums can be a source of progress and development through self-help
Chapter 5: Section 4	Transnational institutions concerned with regulating environmental crimes are contrasted with restorative, self-regulatory and participatory models of development

Comment

Here we suggest three different sites and practices through which entanglement takes place:

■ Ideas – how do ideas about injustice, crime and harm become entangled with ideas about welfare and well-being?

It is through ideas that people come to define what counts as an issue of (in)justice, whose voice or claim counts, and how injustice should be responded to. Ideas on their own can have immense power, as you saw in the example of the struggle against apartheid in Chapter 1, or the growth of concern around environmental issues in Chapter 5. You have seen throughout the book how different ideas about equality and justice have led to the formation of institutions and policies, laws and regulations. But powerful actors – states, corporations, transnational institutions – tend to have an enormous amount of power to define what is a matter of welfare and what a question of crime control. For example, defining those in poverty as potentially 'dangerous' populations tends to open the way for crime control, rather than welfare, measures.

■ Policies and institutions – how can we approach the task of understanding the entanglements between policies and institutions concerned with welfare and those directed towards crime control?

This question alerts us to ways in which welfare policies may take on criminalising tendencies, and criminal justice policies may lead to concerns about welfare and well-being. As Chapter 2 argued, social welfare provision and the institutions through which it is delivered can be imbued with stigmatising, punitive, coercive and repressive dimensions as well as with humanitarian ones.

■ Strategies – how far can institutions solve problems of injustice by regulating behaviour and controlling crime, and how far do such problems rely on other kinds of strategy to produce change and enhance welfare and well-being?

This question highlights the role of regulation and the law as a means of enforcing policies and strategies. Several chapters – particularly Chapter 3 and Chapter 5 – have discussed the criminalisation of those who infringe regulations and laws on equality, health and safety, or environmental pollution. But the discussions suggest that, while laws and regulatory bodies play an important symbolic role, other strategies may also be required – whether this is through positive measures to promote the well-being of workers (Chapter 3) or to encourage greater respect for the welfare of the environment and of those whose lives are intimately involved in caring for it (Chapter 5).

These different kinds of entanglement signify that the relationship between welfare, crime and society is not simple – we can identify different kinds and sorts of entanglement. But does this mean that the differences don't matter? Are they being collapsed in a process of convergence between welfare and crime control strategies? This book has not undertaken the kind of systematic analysis that would enable us definitively to answer whether or not these policies have 'come together' in some way, not least because its authors question whether such a simple narrative of change is helpful for understanding the complexity of these entanglements. But it has pointed to some ways in which social welfare can have punitive consequences, and has indicated some ways in which crime control policies can be said to have welfarist or well-being objectives. Other volumes in this series explore this question in relation to the topics of security (**Cochrane and Talbot, 2008**) and community (**Mooney and Neal, 2009**).

4   Reviewing the evidence

In Chapter 1, Section 7, two of the questions we invited you to consider were:

1   Whose knowledge or experience is presented as evidence?

2   What kinds of evidence are presented, and what might be missing?

These questions are especially important in the context of the focus of this book. Social justice, it has argued, is a mobilising idea, inspiring people to act to bring about social change. And in doing so, different kinds of claims are made to justify change – for example, the claim that a particular group is suffering disadvantage or harm, or that wealth and income are unequally distributed. Similarly, politicians and policymakers tend to make claims about how far poverty has been eradicated or inequalities lessened as a result of government action. The aim of this section is to help you stand back from such claims and say: how do we know? That is, how do we evaluate the evidence we are presented with?

In relation to the first question, it is important to be able to identify the different voices and different speaking positions that are presented as evidence. That is, it may make a difference whether someone is involved in campaigning or protesting, speaking to a newspaper reporter, being interviewed by a social scientist, or writing a personal memoir.

Activity 6.3

Look back over one of the chapters of the book and remind yourself of the visual images, extracts, tables and other sources of evidence that were used. For each, think about whose knowledge or experience is presented. Whose voices can be heard? And what is their speaking position?

Table 6.3 is the beginning of a chart for some of the evidence presented in Chapter 3. In the third column we have suggested some questions you might want to ask about the nature and validity of the evidence. Other issues were raised in the chapter itself.

Table 6.3 Whose evidence?

Chapter 3 examples	Source	Questions raised
Section 2: Extract 3.1	Quotation from government document	How does this extract relate to the whole document? Was the quotation taken out of context? How typical of a general trend is a document depicting policy in Britain?
Section 3: Extract 3.2	Allan's story	How did Marian Barnes, whose research this is drawn from, collect her evidence? What ethical considerations might have been raised in the research?
Section 4.1: Figure 3.7	Images from the film *Ghosts*	What feelings in the viewer are these images intended to produce? How are the images framed to produce a particular effect?
Section 4.2: Extract 3.3	Extract from *The Jungle* by Upton Sinclair	Who is Sinclair, and how did he collect material for his book? This is one person's impression, powerfully described. But how widespread is the phenomenon he describes? And how could we know?
Section 4.4	Quotations from *Nickel and Dimed* by Barbara Ehrenreich	Again, this is a powerful account. How far can we generalise from it?

Comment

It may appear that we have suggested problems with every kind of evidence mentioned in the examples in Table 6.3. But this is not our primary purpose. Rather, we think it is important to try to look behind the evidence you are presented with and ask questions about it – in particular, asking whose evidence it is, and what interests might be at stake. It is also important to ask whose voices have *not* been presented as evidence and what they might have said. This relates back to the notion of 'recognition' introduced in Chapter 1, Section 5: that is, some voices tend to be heard more often in the public domain, while other voices get less recognition, or tend to be dismissed more easily.

Activity 6.4

For this activity, consider the second question about evidence we asked in Chapter 1 – what kinds of evidence are presented, and what might be missing? Look back over previous chapters and try to identify different kinds. For example:

- Evidence about actions and events – what happened?

- Evidence about feelings and impressions – how did people feel?, what did they think?

- Evidence about how significant or widespread something is – how much?, how many?

Comment

In assessing these different kinds of evidence, it is important to bear in mind the issues about 'speaking position' raised in Activity 6.3. For example, in terms of actions and events, or feelings and impressions, whose evidence do we see or hear? And whose accounts may be missing? And, crucially, how might those whose voices are often unheard (e.g. the poor black residents of New Orleans prior to Katrina, in Chapter 4, or those doing care work, in Chapter 3) come to access the public domain?

Throughout this book evidence has been provided from personal accounts or memoirs. Think back to the evidence from Nelson Mandela in Chapter 1; or the accounts of the paramedics caught in the aftermath of Hurricane Katrina in Chapter 4. These are extraordinarily rich and vivid, giving us very important evidence about what it felt like to live in those times in those particular places and to experience those particular forms of injustice. Similar richness can be presented through fiction, as you saw in the inclusion of the extract from Upton Sinclair in Chapter 3. But such accounts are also very personal, and thus may not be 'generalisable'. This means that the conclusions we might reach from reading these accounts may not be valid for other people living in the same place at the same time and experiencing the same form of injustice – we cannot, it seems, move from the particular to the general in a simple way.

This is why other sorts of evidence are also important – especially the kinds of evidence that tell us 'how much' or 'how many' (often called *quantitative* evidence). We could, for example, gather a lot of different accounts — maybe by interviewing or surveying a large number of people — and then try to see what they have in common by looking for how often similar themes, words or answers were repeated. Or we could gather more objective data about the levels of poverty or disadvantage among different populations, comparing incomes, wealth, numbers of years in school, and other kinds of numerical measures. This would provide us with more 'reliable' or 'robust' evidence – that is, evidence that cannot be dismissed as just one person's experience. But inevitably we would lose much of the richness and detail provided by other – more *qualitative* – kinds of evidence.

Similar dilemmas are raised by the use of case studies. A number of these have been presented in preceding chapters, especially in Chapters 3, 4 and 5, in order to give a sense of the detail surrounding particular examples of social injustice or struggles for social justice. Case studies have enabled us to look in depth at particular issues or events; but once again they may not be generalisable. For example, does the evidence about the interaction of poverty and 'race' in New Orleans give us an accurate picture about the position of black populations throughout the USA at the beginning of the twenty-first century? Were the actions of the police force in New Orleans typical of policing in the USA at that time? We cannot know from the evidence presented here.

Why might all this matter? One response is that politicians and policymakers may use all of these kinds of evidence in defining social problems and deciding what to do about them, but that some kinds may be viewed as more 'scientific' than others. This is a problem that social science research faces: that is, how to do research in a way that both captures the richness and complexity of people's lives and experiences, and that also tries to make the findings robust by trying to answer the questions 'how much?' and 'how many?'. A second reason that questions of evidence matter is concerned with power. Collecting evidence takes time and money, and we should therefore be very aware of how this might shape the results. Thinking back to questions of agricultural production raised in Chapter 5, a considerable amount of research has been funded by major companies with an interest in presenting their industry – and their own activities – in the best possible light. Some kinds of research done by social scientists based in universities are more likely to get funded than others, and campaigning organisations may not be able to fund their own research.

Finally, being able to assess the evidence matters to the public at large, and especially to the readers of books such as this one. We hope that this section will have helped you towards becoming more of a 'critical reader' – someone able to reflect on what you are being presented with and to ask questions about it. This means, in particular:

■ noticing what evidence you are being presented with

■ asking questions about 'whose voices' and 'whose experiences' are being presented

■ thinking about what kind of evidence you have been given – whether it is designed to give you a rich and detailed snapshot, or to provide you with robust and generalisable results

■ deciding what else you might need to know.

5   Contestation and change

Throughout this book its authors have emphasised that social justice is a mobilising idea, mobilising individuals and groups to struggle against inequality, poverty, exclusion and harm. Does this mean that claims for social justice will continue to expand as new forms of injustice are made visible and as individuals and groups come to struggle against them?

Looking back over the different contributions to this book we can certainly see some evidence of the idea that there has been an ongoing expansion of claims for social justice. For example, we have seen a growing acceptance of the need to incorporate gender, 'race' and other dimensions of social difference in our understanding of inequality (Chapters 1 and 2). We have seen struggles for recognition on the part of people with physical or mental disabilities, carers and others whose claims tended to be less visible in the historical emphasis on class-based movements against poverty and injustice (Chapter 3). We have also seen the very language of social justice changing, with notions of social inclusion, well-being and freedom from harm entering the vocabulary of both activists and policymakers (Chapters 2 and 4). And Chapter 5 opened up important ideas about how to take account of global poverty and social inequality in our ideas about social justice rather than being limited by a concern about what might be happening in a particular nation state.

Each of these examples suggests ways in which struggles in the name of social justice are expanding, bringing new claims into the public domain and expanding the reach of norms of justice and harm. However, the story of ongoing expansion has also been challenged. Chapters 2 and 3 introduced the idea that the state and other institutions are not only concerned with providing welfare and the means of redressing injustice; they are also in the business of what John Clarke in Chapter 2 calls 'governing populations'. And one way of doing this is by 'tidying away' or smoothing over some of the problems that have previously been the focus of strong social justice movements around poverty and inequality, making such issues less visible and the claims less speakable.

Activity 6.5

Look back at Chapter 2, Section 4.3 on 'Managing and governing populations'. Then think about some of the shifts in how injustice is discussed. Some examples you could look at can be found in:

- Chapter 2, Section 6: From inequality to exclusion

- Chapter 3, Section 2: Well-being, harm and social justice

- Chapter 4, Section 4: Review: misrecognition, disrespect and the politics of fear.

In what ways do you think these examples limit, rather than expand, the meaning of social justice and shape what kinds of struggle are likely to be viewed as legitimate? For example, how does the shift of language from inequality to social exclusion change the meaning of social justice? What kinds of claim might the idea of social exclusion open up; and what kinds of claim might it close down, or make less possible? How might the categorisation of particular population groups as problem populations limit responses to their claims for social justice?

Comment

The focus on social inclusion and well-being rather than poverty or inequality can be viewed as positive, in that it opens up questions of recognition as well as redistribution (see Chapter 1, Section 5 for a discussion of these concepts). But there are also potential problems in the shift of focus to cultural, rather than material, forms of disadvantage. That is, problems are assumed to be something to do with the person or population concerned rather than the wider society – they may lack particular skills, their childcare practices may be deficient, they may have the 'wrong' sorts of attitudes, and so on. As such, the dominant policy response in many mature welfare states is in terms of strategies to promote recognition through social inclusion rather than strategies to redistribute resources.

As a result of these processes of redefinition and re-categorisation, poverty and disadvantage come to be viewed through a narrowed, rather than expanded, prism. In many nations, questions of injustice and inequality are in the process of being sidelined from political and policy debate. Such problems are assumed to have been mainly solved, through the activities of welfare states and other institutions. Where such problems exist, they are subject to the kinds of 'othering' raised in

Chapter 2 and debated in Chapter 4, Section 4, becoming associated with particular places and particular people – migrants, the inhabitants of slums, people whose skills and attitudes do not fit them for the 'modern' world, and so on. It is these populations, and the places with which they are associated, that are assumed to create their own problems.

But we cannot leave this debate without revisiting the ideas of global social justice introduced in Chapter 1 and developed Chapter 5. In Chapter 5, Allan Cochrane and Reece Walters ask us to make a number of shifts in how we think about the boundaries of what we mean by social justice, both as a normative and as a mobilising idea. First, they ask us to shift the scale. If, as Chapter 2 argued, welfare states formed one kind of institutional response to claims for social justice that took place within specific nation states, how can we envisage responses that take account of global issues and struggles?

Second, Cochrane and Walters bring to our attention other kinds of social justice claim than those dominant in the industrial economies of the West. Access to clean water, basic health care and protection from environmental harms are very different from the kinds of demands that helped shape the development of welfare states. Third, they turn on its head the idea that it is those in poverty who are the cause of their own problems by focusing on the role of the rich as the perpetrators of social harms, and by depicting those living in urban slums not as 'problem populations' but as a potential source of dynamism and change.

6   The politics of social justice

As we have noted in earlier sections of this chapter, the authors of this book have addressed different dimensions of social justice. But there is no simple story – no book-wide definition of what 'counts' as social justice, how we would know whether we have achieved it, or which claims for social justice should be viewed as legitimate claims. This is because we can understand social justice only by debating wider themes and issues – the nature of contestation and change, the relationship between the national and the global, the different dimensions of inequality and exclusion, the changing role of states, and the role of global institutions in a changing world.

This is why this book has as its subtitle 'welfare, crime and society'. The chapters have given different interpretations of the relationship between social welfare policies and crime control strategies. A focus on entanglement can be a helpful way of transcending simple stories of change or progress in which social justice is viewed as an ongoing struggle that is gradually being won. The idea of entanglement alerts us to the shadowy dangers or limitations of what appear to be fruitful and positive measures. This is not a case for not pursuing such measures; but we think that holding on to their potential ambiguity is important. Rather than providing a story about the historical development of social justice as an idea or about the growth of welfare states and social policies, the authors of this book have explored some of the dilemmas associated with trying to bring about change towards more socially just societies. But despite the difficulties and dilemmas, the work of challenging ideas that 'naturalise' particular patterns of inequality, and resisting the criminalisation of those who try to mobilise social change, are crucial elements shaping the contemporary politics of social justice.

7 References

Cochrane, A. and Talbot, D. (eds) (2008) *Security: Welfare, Crime and Society*, Maidenhead, Open University Press/Milton Keynes, The Open University.

Mooney, G. and Neal, S. (eds) (2009) *Community: Welfare, Crime and Society*, Maidenhead, Open University Press/Milton Keynes, The Open University.

Acknowledgements

Grateful acknowledgement is made to the following sources:

Cover

Copyright © Ian Waldie/Getty Images.

Chapter 1

Text

Extract 1.2: Borger, J. (2006) 'Civil rights heroes may get pardons', *The Guardian*, 4 April 2006. Copyright © Guardian News & Media Limited 2006.

Figures

Figure 1.1 left: Copyright © Hulton-Deutsch Collection/Corbis; Figure 1.1 right: Copyright © Fabian Bimmer/AP/PA Photos; Figure 1.2: by kind permission of Save the Children; Figure 1.5: Copyright © Tony Harris/PA Archive/PA Photos; Figure 1.4: Copyright © Bill Hudson/AP/PA Photos; Figure 1.5: Copyright © Tom Pietrask; Figure 1.6: Copyright © Reuters/Corbis.

Chapter 2

Figures

Figure 2.1: Copyright © John Stillwell/PA Archive/PA Photos; Figure 2.3: Guildhall Library, City of London; Figure 2.4: Hulton Archive/Getty Images; Figure 2.5: Hulton Archive/Getty Images; Figure 2.6 top: Copyright © Tom Craig/PhotographersDirect; Figure 2.6 centre: Copyright © Graham Turner/Getty Images; Figure 2.6 bottom: Copyright © John Harris, Report Digital; Figure 2.7: Copyright © Martin Rickett/PA Archive/PA Photos.

Chapter 3

Figures

Figure 3.1 top: Copyright © John Harris/Report Digital; Figure 3.1 centre: Copyright © Jess Hurd/Report Digital; Figure 3.1 bottom: Copyright © Paul Carter/Report Digital; Figure 3.2: Copyright © Michael Stephens/PA Archives/PA Photos; Figure 3.3: Copyright © Howie Twiner; Figure 3.4: Copyright © Paul Doyle/Photofusion; Figure 3.5: Copyright © Tom Olin; Figure 3.6: Copyright © Jess Hurd/Report Digital; Figure 3.7: Ronald Grant Archive; Figure 3.8: Library of Congress, Prints & Photographs Division, reproduction numbers LC-USZ62-52728 and LC-USZ62-52729; Figure 3.9: Copyright © Jess Hurd/Report Digital.

Chapter 4

Text

Extract 4.1: Bradshaw, L. and Slonsky, L.B. (2005) 'The real heroes and sheroes of New Orleans', *Socialist Worker Online*, 9 September 2005 www.socialistworker.org.

Figures

Figure 4.2 top: Copyright © Greater New Orleans Community Data Center www.gnocdc.org; Figure 4.2 bottom: Copyright © David J Phillip/AP/PA Photos; Figure 4.3 top left: Copyright Dave Martin/AP/PA Photos; Figure 4.3 top right: Copyright © Jason Reed/Reuters/Corbis; Figure 4.3 bottom left: Copyright © Michael Ainsworth/Dallas Morning News/Corbis; Figure 4.3 bottom right: Copyright © Michael Ainsworth/Dallas Morning News/Corbis; Figure 4.4 left: Copyright © Jacques Brinon/AP/PA Photos; Figure 4.4 top right: Copyright © Reuters/Corbis; Figure 4.4 bottom right: Copyright © Sipa Press/Rex Features; Figure 4.5: Copyright © Raymond Kleboe/Hulton Archive/Getty Images; Figure 4.6: Copyright © Sean Damer.

Chapter 5

Text

Extract 5.2: Muiruri, M. (2006) 'Kenya Loses Sh70m to biopirates', *Kenya Times*, 29 August 2006; Extract 5.3: Ogodo, O. and Vidal, J. (2007) 'Drained of life', *The Guardian*, 14 February 2007. Copyright © Guardian News & Media Ltd 2007.

Figures

Figure 5.1 top: Copyright © NOAA/Science Photo Library; Figure 5.2 top left: Copyright © Karen Kasmauski/Corbis; Figure 5.2 top right: Copyright © Gregg Newton/Corbis; Figure 5.2 bottom left: Copyright © SR/TS/Keystone USA/Rex Features; Figure 5.2 bottom right: Copyright © KPA/Zuma/Rex Features; Figure 5.3: Copyright © 2006 SASI Group (University of Sheffield) and Mark Newman (University of Michigan) www.worldmapper.org; Figure 5.4 top: Copyright © Jon Freeman/Rex Features; Figure 5.4 bottom: Copyright © Antti Aimo-Koivisto/Rex Features; Figure 5.5: Copyright © Rex Features; Figure 5.6: Copyright © Simon Maina/Getty Images; Figure 5.7: Copyright © Rebecca Naden/PA Archive/PA Photos.

Every effort has been made to contact copyright holders. If any have been inadvertently overlooked the publishers will be pleased to make the necessary arrangements at the first opportunity.

Index